WITNESS

&

LEGACY

MINNESOTA MUSEUM OF AMERICAN ART • SAINT PAUL, MINNESOTA
JANUARY 29-MAY 14, 1995

WITNESS

&

LEGACY

CONTEMPORARY

ART

ABOUT THE

HOLOCAUST

EDITED BY STEPHEN C. FEINSTEIN

LERNER PUBLICATIONS COMPANY

MINNEAPOLIS, MINNESOTA

Front cover:
Edith Altman
The Paradox of Creativity
from *Reclaiming the Symbol,* 1992
Photo construction
30 x 48

Back cover:
Judith Goldstein
Vilno Ghetto, 1994
Mixed media
51 x 30

Page 2:
Debbie Teicholz
Untitled from *Prayer by the Wall,*
1991
Photograph
35 x 64

ISBN: 0-8225-3148-8
Library of Congress catalog card number: 94-079015

Manufactured in the United States of America

1 2 3 4 5 6 - I/JR - 00 99 98 97 96 95

TABLE OF CONTENTS

FOREWORD

It is almost too horrible to contemplate, but nonetheless true, that the Holocaust will stand as the modern era's signature misachievement, the twentieth century's contribution to humanity. Modern government, modern science, modern industry, modern culture produced not the utopia they promised but, rather, the "final solution." These institutions, in which we must still place our faith, either caused or failed to stop an unprecedented type of mass murder.

This is also the century in which artists understand that culture is entwined in a society's value system. To paraphrase Jerome Witkin's statement in this catalog, we will be made to answer: When the Holocaust was over, what did the culture do to diagnose and treat this self-inflicted wound? If it is true that we are now in a postmodern era and that progress has stopped, it may be because our culture has not fully come to terms with the Holocaust, the rot at the center of our civilization, and will not have the heart to continue until it does.

It is our intention with *Witness and Legacy* to announce a contemporary movement, the phenomenon of American artists of various experiential perspectives, using various strategies, working today to bring the Holocaust into our cultural dialogue. I am in awe of the courage of these witnesses and their legacy, the sons and daughters and those who are drawn by conscience to such a painful subject. They feel compelled, even duty-bound, to create these artworks, and while the work may give them some solace, it can never finally give them peace. Nonetheless, all of us, the artists and the audience, must do the work of understanding how the Holocaust happened and what it has done to our humanity.

Paul Spencer
Co-curator of *Witness and Legacy*
Minnesota Museum of American Art

ACKNOWLEDGMENTS

Witness and Legacy is an exhibition that poses a profound and fundamental question: How does one make art about such a moment of history as the Holocaust? Where do the threads of memory, experience, personal creativity and respect for those who perished intersect as a work of art? As co-curator Stephen Feinstein notes in his essay, within the realm of art, the Holocaust era may be just now emerging.

I want to express my gratitude to Professor Feinstein and his colleagues Yehudit Shendar of the University of Minnesota and Matthew Baigell of Rutgers University, who contributed essays to this catalog. Paul Spencer, the museum's associate curator, has worked tirelessly on the exhibition. I also want to recognize the significant contributions of project director and co-curator Lynette Henderson, formerly with the museum's education department, Beth Richardson, the museum's development director, William R. Hegeman, communications director, and Eunice Haugen, registrar.

I also wish to acknowledge the contributions of the *Witness and Legacy* partnership committee: Samuel H. Asher, Maureen Beck, professors Scott and Lynn Bryce, Sheila Field, Dr. Robert Fisch, Reva Rosenbloom, Ruth Stein, Ruth Ann Weiss, Anita White and Dr. Carol Wirtschafter.

I also want to thank our sponsor committee members who played key roles in making the dream of this exhibition a reality: Reva Rosenbloom, Beverly and Dick Fink, DeeDee and Dick Harris, Judy and Bunny Kuller, Sheila and Stephen E. Lieberman, Rhoda and Don Mains and Mimi and David Sanders. In addition, the board of trustees of the Minnesota Museum of American Art has been unstinting in its support of this exhibition and related programs.

Finally, I want to thank Harry J. Lerner and the staff of Lerner Publications Company for making this catalog possible.

Ruth Stevens Appelhof, Ph.D.
Director
Minnesota Museum of American Art

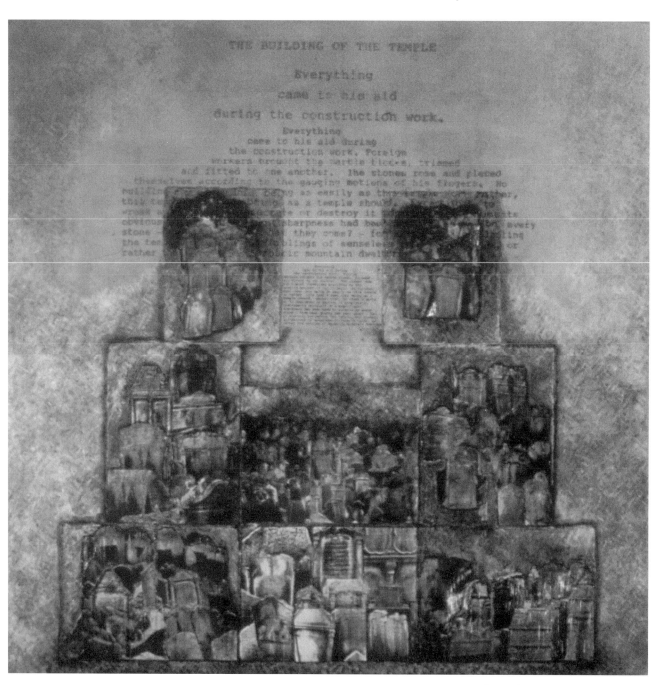

Susan Erony
The Building of the Temple, 1993
Photos, acrylic, xerox transfer
on canvas
44 x 44

WITNESS AND LEGACY

The Golgotha of modern mankind is Auschwitz. The cross, the Roman gallows, was replaced by the gas chamber.

—*Ignasz Maybaum*

All is not vanity, all is horror.

—*Rico LeBrun*

Why this determination to show "everything" in pictures? A word, a glance, silence itself communicates more and better... the Holocaust is not a subject like all others. It imposes certain limits.[1]

—*Elie Wiesel*

The Holocaust is a subject that on the surface seems to defy artistic representation. The dehumanization, humiliation and mass murder of European Jewry by the Nazis was an event of unparalleled proportions. Other groups such as Romani and Sinti peoples (Gypsies), Jehovah's Witnesses, homosexuals, political prisoners and opponents to the Nazi regime became part of the world of the concentration and death camps. However, in the diabolical world of Nazi race theory, only the Jews and most of the Gypsies were chosen for genocide.[2]

Art had a lot to do with the Nazi regime and has a logical relationship with the Holocaust, despite the aesthetic and ethical problems that are raised for artists in the aftermath of such horror. Hitler himself aspired to become an artist but failed admission to art school. *Mein Kampf,* Hitler's 1923 plan for himself and the world, denounced modernism, abstract and Dadaist art as an affront to civilization. Hitler's artistic tastes can be judged by his favorite work of art, a realistic, military World War I painting by Elk Eber, *The Last Hand Grenade.*

Six hundred works of art representing such heroic themes were hung for the *Grosse Deutsche Kunstausstellung* (Great German Art Exhibition), which opened in Munich on July 18, 1937. A day later, the first of many "degenerate" *(Entartete Kunst)* art shows was opened just across the from the Great German Art Exhibition. These shows, which may have drawn the largest crowds in museum history, juxtaposed "degenerate" art, "influenced by the Jews," to the Aryan ideal as expressed in painting and sculpture. Many important avant-garde works from the Weimar period were destroyed as part of the war on culture. In 1942, Hitler even had three of his own paintings seized from private collections and destroyed.[3]

These actions in Munich signaled the start of the Nazi attack on culture, an attack that ultimately could be considered a war against imagination. The attack on imagination was a prelude to what mutated into genocide on a massive scale. The scale of Jewish death was so great that the aftermath of World War II left the Jews and others searching for a word to describe it. The preferred Hebrew word was *Shoah,* meaning calamity, but having a special reference to earlier attempts to destroy the Jews during the biblical period. The word Holocaust came into use during the late 1950s. It too is laden with religious implications, as its Greek origins suggest a "burnt offering." More and more, Shoah is the preferred descriptive word among Jews, as Holocaust has been used in reference to non-Jewish victims as well as to other horrible events in the post-1945 period.[4]

Attempts by artists to grapple with the catastrophe that would become the Shoah began in the earliest days of the Nazi regime. It was a movement that became visible during Hitler's rise and concentration of power. Marc Chagall's *White Crucifixion,* a response to Kristallnacht— "The Night of Broken Glass," remains the icon among many paintings that described Jewish suffering before 1939. Chagall used the theme of a crucified "Jewish" Jesus set against vignettes of Jewish persecution that unfolded in the Nazi era. Artists like Yankel Adler and Ben Shahn produced strong responses to Jewish and other persecution during World War II. Both Jewish and non-Jewish artists who were interned in concentration camps and perished produced artistic legacies of their victimization. A strong postwar response appeared from the pallet of many important artists. Among postwar abstractionists, Rico LeBrun, a non-Jew, insisted that "the Holocaust was a subject that no serious artist could neglect...."[5] The American painter Leonard Baskin, LeBrun's colleague and friend, described his approach to the subject as confronting "the mind-curdling reality of the least human of human endeavors, and in paintings and drawings of dissolution, dismemberment and incineration he is saying, all is not vanity, all is horror."[6]

In the 1960s the subject of the Holocaust was not avoided, but appeared infrequently in art, except in the realm of building public memorials, principally at the sites of destruction in Europe. Artists responded very much like survivors themselves who decided against talking about the event. During the 1970s and 1980s, a new generation of artists emerged who, with a sensitivity toward the subject, attempted to grapple with the difficulties of art after such a monstrous period of destruction. There can be many conundrums and taboos. One is when, as Elie Wiesel has said, "merchants of images and the brokers of language would set themselves up to speak for the victims."[7] Another was described by Frank Rich when he noted that the numerous Holocaust memorials in Europe and the United States share one common trait: impermanence.[8] Raul Hilberg has gone even further and has described much of the memorial architecture as "kitsch" or "done without taste, without awareness."[9]

Despite such conditions, especially the issue of artists simply trying to "reproduce" a memory of an event they did not experience and competition with the archival photographic record, the quest for a visual language and a means to convey memory continues. Like early Christian artists who tried to imagine the Crucifixion of Jesus, contemporary artists are trying to artistically convey the horror and memory of the Holocaust.

The quest, in a certain sense, is for a new language with new symbols and new metaphors. Primo Levi understood this well, when writing about his experiences he said: "Daily language is for the description of daily experience, but here is another world, here one would need a language 'of the other world.'"[10]

It is also a form of memory that treads on sacred soil: "In the Jewish tradition, death is a private, intimate matter, and we are forbidden to transform it into a spectacle. If that is true for an individual, it is six million times more true for one of the largest communities of the dead in history."[11]

The Holocaust, as *Witness and Legacy* tries to demonstrate, need not necessarily produce a type of artistic response connected with horror. Horror is a familiar subject in art. Medieval and Renaissance artists portrayed the grim face of the Black Death and a landscape of horror caused by war. Grünewald's *Isenheim Altarpiece,* a masterpiece of the Northern Renaissance, has been referred to by many artists as "a Holocaust work of art," in the way it depicts the horror of the Crucifixion of Jesus. Goya depicted massacres of civilians and atrocities of war. World War I provided an impetus for artists to become involved in burning political questions. George Grosz, Otto Dix, Max Ernst, Salvador Dali and Pablo Picasso, to name a few, made incomparable political statements and reflected on the violence of the century in many of their works. Picasso's *Guernica,* with its specific reference to the civil war in Spain, later became a metaphor for the entire century's violence.

The contemporary world's exceptional focus on politics and rights for minorities, with the lurking fear of brutalization close to the surface, has produced a substantial number of exhibitions that deal with subjects such as feminism, AIDS, homosexuality, black consciousness and the new specter of genocide as seen in Bosnia. Installation art has served as a particularly responsive bridge between the artistic community and political issues. These shows, however, may not solve the question of permanence.

Permanence is part of the United States Holocaust Memorial Museum, which opened in Washington, D.C., in April 1993. Here the architect, James T. Freed, created a major interior space dedicated to telling the story of the Holocaust, a space where art plays a role. Outside the building is Joel Shapiro's abstract bronze sculpture *Loss and Regeneration,* suggesting a house turned upside down. Ellsworth Kelly's white on white *Memorial* installation creates a silent space between scenes of horror for the museum visitor. Sol LeWitt's *Consequence* is a large work applied directly to the museum walls with a theme of variations on black and colored squares. Richard Serra's *Gravity,* a 10-inch-thick, 10-foot-square standing slab of Cor-ten steel, is an interior sculpture in the Hall of Witnesses.

These works have all received mixed reviews. They are all abstract and according to Paul Richard, art critic for the *Washington Post,* were "unnecessary, distorted and misguided,"[12] as they could suggest violence anywhere. Ken Johnson, writing in *Art in America,* described the museum's approach to art as "so much less daring," especially given the cutting-edge work by artists like Robert Morris, Christian Boltanski, Jonathan Borofsky, Anselm Kiefer, Sue Coe and others.[13] The debate will continue.

Witness and Legacy examines a spectrum of Holocaust-related art produced by some American artists during the last twenty years.[14] The mediums include painting, sculpture, photography, graphic design, needlepoint and multimedia installation art. The wide variety of work that has been produced is exceptional in scope, but untested in thematic presentation.

In addition to division by medium, *Witness and Legacy* deals with what might be called "different generations" of the Holocaust—artists from different backgrounds who bring to the subject their unique perspectives because of their relationship to the event.

One-third of the artists represented are Holocaust survivors themselves who have worked as professional artists. Children of survivors, sometimes called "the second generation," make up the second group. The third group are artists not directly connected with the Holocaust who have developed a sensitivity toward the subject because of their humanitarianism and empathy and attempt to understand the event and convey it to others through art.

Survivors all share a special vision of having been victims during the Holocaust. The other artists cannot claim the same vision. Survivors possess memories that other artists can comprehend only in indirect ways. In some respect, the only "authentic" Holocaust art may be the art of survivors. Artists such as Judith Goldstein, Samuel Bak, Kitty Klaidman and Netty Vanderpol experienced the terror of the ghettos and the death camps. Their art is somewhere between visual memoir and metaphoric memory.

Sometimes art is created as a coping mechanism. Questions of aesthetics may exist, creating a tension between memory and witnessing versus a purely artistic approach to the subject.

Edith Altman, Gabrielle Rossmer and Gerda Meyer-Bernstein fall into a category between survivors and second-generation artists. Coming to the United States as children just before the war, they escaped extended ghettoization and later horrors, but carry with them some of the burdens of survivors and certainly part of the trauma of their parents' victimization and near destruction.

For many members of the second generation, art and literature are mediums for expressing their special relationship to the Holocaust and to their parents. The second generation does not have a direct memory of ghettos and death camps. But they may carry the memory and burdens of their parents' trauma, conveyed directly or indirectly. After the camps were liberated, many survivors made new lives for themselves in Israel, Western Europe or the United States. Some bore no outward traces of their dehumanization. Others suffered a great deal in a way that was conveyed directly or indirectly to their children. Some things could not disappear: numbers tattooed on parents' forearms, screams in the night, the absence of grandparents, uncles, aunts and other family members and dark shadows in a family past that would not be talked about.

For the second generation, art provided an appropriate entry for questions of memory, absence, presence and identity. The visual representations of the second generation mark the continued impact of the terrible period of the Holocaust on a generation that did not directly experience it. These are children who cannot conceive of their existence without the vast imprint of the Holocaust upon it. In this exhibition, Joyce Lyon, Pier Marton, Gabrielle Rossmer, Art Spiegelman, Debbie Teicholz and Mindy Weisel are representative of this group. Their mediums of expression represent the breadth of the art: painting, photography, video, installation art and the comic strip.

Artists who were not directly involved with the Holocaust have also attempted to enter the subject. This is probably the most difficult road. The stimulus may be some knowledge about the Holocaust itself or analogies made between the Holocaust and contemporary events that demand an emotional or political response in art. Artists may be Jews or non-Jews. Rico Le-Brun, a non-Jew known for his Crucifixion scenes, suggested that artists had to deal with the Holocaust. This "outsider" generation (sometimes called "empathizers") has important ethical boundaries to consider when approaching the subject. The art of this group cannot be "memory," for they did not experience the event itself. It may be an interpretation (derived from a sense of vulnerability as a Jew or artist), a historical narrative, reflections on place, absence and presence, a Proustian stimulus to a book, photograph or film, confrontation with a survivor or neo-Nazi or simply a confrontation with the impenetrability of the subject. The greater question at hand, however, may not be the Holocaust, but an attempt to penetrate the nature of man and seek light through the darkness of the late twentieth century.

In *Witness and Legacy,* eight artists are represented who have no direct connection with the event. Mauricio Lasansky, a native of Argentina and now professor emeritus at the University of Iowa, produced *The Nazi Drawings* during the mid-1960s. The thirty large works in this series made a strong impact when shown at the Philadelphia Museum of Art in 1967 and later at the Whitney Museum in New York. The series *Kaddish* represents an ongoing digression into the dignity, self-destructiveness and suffering of mankind. The title is derived from the Jewish prayer for the dead, the text of which is an affirmation of God.

Larry Rivers has done occasional paintings as responses to reading Primo Levi and seeing Nazi photographs of Jews awaiting selection at Auschwitz-Birkenau. Several paintings were done as commissions. The Holocaust is not a major part of Rivers' oeuvre. The Holocaust well fits Rivers' larger themes that have dealt with political questions of other groups and how memory is made and revised.

Jerome Witkin is an American-born Jewish artist whose realistic paintings have increasingly dealt with the Holocaust. Among his recent large and often frightening works are *Hitler as an Usher, The Butcher's Helper,* and the painting featured in this show, *The Beating Station, Berlin, 1933.* Witkin uses historical information to produce narrative works that focus, with their metaphoric realism, on the brutality of Nazism. This violence was not invisible, as the beatings and the rape of a Jewish woman on the streets

of Berlin suggest. Witkin implicitly brings the viewer to contemplate religious issues connected with the Holocaust, as the title, bearing within it the word "station," can refer to a deportation point and the stations of the cross in the Passion of Jesus.

Arnold Trachtman is a Boston-born artist who grew up during World War II and has strong memories of American anti-Semitism. Utilizing a disjointed technique that may be compared with montage in filmmaking, Trachtman depicts historical events, such as Neville Chamberlain's "Peace in Our Time" speech after the October 1938 Munich Agreement, and its consequences— the production of mounds of bodies and material debris from the victims. Trachtman has also produced pop-art-like paintings about the complicity of German industry in building the death camps and the use of slave labor as the basis for their profits.

Pearl Hirshfield is a Chicago-born installation artist whose life has been heavily involved in political and social issues and whose art reflects a necessity of involvement. Her installations have dealt with far-ranging subjects such as McCarthyism, feminist issues, abortion rights, police brutality, the Ku Klux Klan and cultural differences. She often opts for theatrical presentations in installations, utilizing disparate elements such as mirrors, sound systems, water fountains and texts of diaries recorded on audio tape. Her installation in this show, *Shadows of Auschwitz,* is an environment of memory with negative and positive spaces that recreate part of the road to death at Auschwitz. In this provocative work, viewers become victims as actual Auschwitz camp numbers reflect on their own images.

Jeffrey Wolin, a professor at Indiana University, has developed a unique photographic approach to the Holocaust. Wolin recently completed a Guggenheim Fellowship that involved photographing and videotaping accounts of Holocaust survivors. His photographs show survivors as they look today, for the most part in the safe and apparently "normal" physical environments of their homes or workplaces. However, the menacing past experiences, traumas and suffering, plus the persistence of memory, is imposed on the photograph by a textual narration of the subject's history. The stories are intimate and recall the absolute horror of the subjects' humiliation, near destruction and survival.

Marlene Miller and Shirley Samberg provide two varying approaches to Holocaust-related sculpture. Miller, a professor at Bucks County Community College outside of Philadelphia, creates sculpture from papier-mâché and other materials that is reminiscent of medieval tableaux. Miller worked in puppet theaters, and the fascination about such creativity provided her with an inroad to sculpture about the Holocaust. In addition, while seeing Claude Lanzmann's documentary film *Shoah,* she was struck by testimony that indicated that the SS guards forced inmates to call the dead bodies *figuren* or "puppets." One of her large sculptures (not in this show) depicts three crucified figures, two men and a woman, with *Arbeit Macht Frei* (Work Makes You Free) written in place of the traditional INRI of Crucifixion scenes. *Schlafwagen: Who Will Say Kaddish For Them?* is a meditation on the absence of honor for the dead during the Holocaust and a sardonic interpretation of a sleeping car from the German *schlafwagen.* This sculptural piece is also loaded with the debris produced by the death camps: shoes, photographs, religious objects and aspects of bodies themselves. Miller's creations are suggestive of the "plastic" works of the Polish artist and theater producer Jozef Szajna, who, as an Auschwitz survivor himself, sees civilization constantly trying to forget the meaning of Arbeit Macht Frei, the cruel joke that greeted inmates as they arrived at the death camps.

Shirley Samberg's works can be read with a Holocaust context, but their metaphorical connections are more tenuous. Using glue, paint, sand, stucco and dirt on wet burlap, Samberg's *Wrappings* represent groupings of survivors from any type of disaster. Devoid of both faces and normal limbs, they appear as specters. Yet at the same time, they convey a sense of tragedy that is all too familiar to the contemporary world. The human form with absence of face and hands also conforms to limitations imposed on traditional Jewish and Islamic art from the commandment against false idols.

Robert Barancik and Susan Erony take two radically different approaches to the Holocaust theme. Barancik is a Philadelphia graphic artist who is deeply American in his Jewish identity and was removed from the Holocaust. In 1990 Barancik attended an artists' retreat in Vermont that sensitized him to a more open discussion of the subject. Since then, he has produced two small books of folded messages entitled *Kvitl Shoah.* Each work contains six original cards that are made as collages and hand-painted in colorful gouache. The inner spaces of each card contain meditations about the Holocaust. These works derive a great amount of their content from biblical imagery, both Jewish and Christian. But the main focus is Jewish absence and the deep intergenerational effect on all Jews as potential victims: "Jewish bones leach unseen into the hard old world soil. Crematoria smoke vanishes into the blue lungs of empty sky...." reads one of the messages.

Erony, living in Boston, is involved in a large project about the Holocaust based on her sense of responsibility as a Jewish artist to retell the story visually. Her specific focus is the technological aspects of modern barbarism, dehumanization and statements against genocide and its recent variant, "ethnic cleansing." Additional works in the series deal with destroyed Jewish communities—Lodz, Prague and others. Some of the materials are photographic, while others are in some respects relics of the Jews themselves. Erony's visit to Lodz, Poland, in 1989 came after a fire at the only synagogue there. Burned prayer books were being thrown away. She took them and integrated the charred remains into several works as memorials to the victims. Erony is sensitive to certain limits of politically oriented art. The work must always be art and avoid trivialization.

THE SURVIVOR ARTIST

A document that survives from the art jury committee in the Vilna ghetto from March 16, 1943, indicated approval for exhibiting twenty-seven sketches by "S. Bak (9 years old)."[15] Since then, Samuel Bak's entire life has been involved with the difficult memories of the Holocaust. He survived physically, but only barely on an emotional level.

His art began as abstract expressionism, with some similarities to Rothko's altar-like works. By the 1970s, however, Bak was working in surrealistic landscapes with both a Renaissance pallet and Magritte-like irony in most of his works. However, the major focus was not a flippant humor, rather a serious attempt to deal with his survival. His work may be likened to a healing art or reflect the deep tragedy of the powerlessness of ghetto existence. In *The Observers,* from 1973, his figures appear like concentration camp survivors, cut off at the shoulder. The have no limbs and are juxtaposed to constructive-like paper cutouts and chess pawns. *The Ghetto* (1976) appears as a destroyed town set within a tomb in the earth in the shape of a Star of David. Variations of this work have integrated Judaic themes of Sabbath or *yahrzeit* (memorial) candles, expressing a deep grieving process the artist continues to go through. In his still-life scenes, the objects are dysfunctional. In other paintings, angels, often bearers of biblical prophecy and rescue, have leather wings that seem not to work or are themselves in chains. Many of his works refer to the obliteration of the Ten Commandments. *That Is the Question,* a 1989 still life of broken objects, reminds one of Hamlet's soliloquy and the words that came earlier, "To be or not to be," which was part of daily survival in the ghetto. The layers of destruction that Bak paints are set against beautiful landscape backgrounds and calm skies, references to the isolation of the victims and perhaps the complacency of the world of the onlookers.

Living now near Boston, Bak continues to paint on an even grander scale, and his works have drawn in more symbols of the past and contemporary worlds and their illusions. Pears, wine bottles, broken clocks and clocks, chess pieces and Hebrew letters are symbols that appear in various states of decomposition in Bak's works, conveying in their own way layerings of pain for the viewer. Bak sees an absolute need to use the metaphor of surrealism as a way of confronting the Holocaust. He has written:

> My reluctance to deal with these subjects in a direct way must have multiple reasons. Objectively, documents, films and memoirs seem to me more eloquent than a painter's creation. And yet they seldom achieve more than a faint echo of the reality that they try to describe. One might possibly solve this by way of a meaningful transfiguration, but the forms or subjective expressionism, brought to their maximal development by the advent of two World Wars, are at present exhausted.[16]

Viewers will note that Bak's paintings come exceptionally close to creating an entirely new visual vocabulary for interpreting the Holocaust, through both his own suffering and as a metaphor for specific and universalized disturbances.

Judith Goldstein is also a survivor of the Vilna ghetto and Stutthof and Buchenwald concentration camps. Her father was killed, although her mother and brother survived. Most of her relatives perished at Ponar, a massacre site outside Vilna, which, like Babi Yar outside of Kiev, for many years had no commemorative marker. Goldstein's art possesses a certain naive style, which has been used also by Ilex Beller in France, Pearl Hessing in England and the American-Jewish artist Harry Lieberman, who was not a survivor but painted some interesting Holocaust paintings. This style, when related to the theme of the Holocaust, is sometimes disarming to the viewer, as the power of the subject is in some conflict with the apparent lightness of the medium. Goldstein's collages are her memories and hopes as she constantly reflects back on her period of captivity. In *Crematory,* the oven and smokestack appear as a modern icon, with visions of human heads in the smoke. *Vilno Ghetto* was based on symbols in a ring Goldstein's father made in the ghetto from a silver coin. She managed to keep it, despite searches that necessitated giving up every other possession as she went through Stutthof and Buchenwald. The collage utilizes the Hebrew letters vov and gimmel, the abbreviation for the Vilna ghetto, as a title for a triangle that incorporates symbols of oppression and dehumanization with a few elements of hope. *Vilno Ghetto* also contains references to the musical life of the ghetto and to Goldstein's memories of the choir conductor, Dumashkin, who was later killed. Goldstein herself has also explored musical approaches to the Holocaust, having written several songs about her experiences.

Netty Schwartz Vanderpol was born in Amsterdam and was thirteen years old when Nazi Germany invaded the Netherlands. She was a classmate of Anne Frank, whose diary is one of the most celebrated works of modern literature. In 1943, Vanderpol and her family were deported to Westerbork concentration camp and then Terezin, north of Prague. Vanderpol was placed on several deportation trains for

Auschwitz, only to be removed at the last minute. In February 1945, she and a group of fellow inmates from Terezin were sent to Switzerland in exchange for German prisoners of war, the only such exchange of the war.

Vanderpol started doing needlepoint in 1984, and it became a vehicle for dealing with her emotions and "guilt of survival," a form of therapy. Her work represents an abstract type of art, with a collective title for her work, *Every Stitch a Memory*. Each work deals with various "textures of grief," as she describes it, and is both art for viewing and therapy for the artist. Some works contain direct Holocaust imagery, such as the Star of David with the Dutch word *Jood*, barbed wire, concentration camp numbers, vignettes of flowers that grew near the perimeter fence at Terezin and train tracks. One work, *All the King's Horses and All the King's Men*, is a needlepoint design that includes a broken mirror, a testimony to the broken life of her mother, who later was a victim of Alzheimer's disease but still remembered the camps. The broken mirror is also a metaphor for her own broken life.

Vanderpol's medium, needlepoint, is unique and is often difficult for the art critic to approach. Her focus within the medium is abstraction, and her works have been compared to some of the chromaticists of the abstract expressionist movement of the post-1945 period. Each work contains very quiet and controlled symbols and perhaps an inner rage. Powerful textures of the yarn itself are woven into evocative designs. One cannot go away from Vanderpol's work without the feeling of having witnessed a vast disturbance, which may be Holocaust-specific in most works, but is also a universal expression of grief. As a medium, needlepoint is also specifically feminine, and in this case it is raised to the level of a higher contemporary art form.

During the Holocaust, Kitty Klaidman was a hidden child. She was protected at first by a Christian neighbor, Jan Velicky, who then found refuge for her family with the Drinas family, who were farmers. The Klaidmans lived for two years in an attic space of the farmhouse. Klaidman's visual memory of her youth, therefore, is heavily involved in recalling horrible and long periods of anxiety. *Hidden Memories* is a series of paintings that focus on these attic spaces. They carry with them some ominous overtones, but

also a sense of abstraction that can produce a non-Holocaust interpretation emphasizing painterly aspects of the works. *Ghost Games* is a series that juxtaposes the view down circular staircases with old family photographs. *Childhood Revisited* is a mixed-media series that peers at the past as if through shaded and aged photographs. One might detect in these works some similarity of landscape with that of Joyce Lyon's work, and the use of photographs evokes some comparisons with Christian Boltanski's utilization of photographs in installations.

Gabrielle Rossmer did not have memories of attic hiding. However, her evading the Holocaust by coming to America just before the outbreak of World War II did not have a totally happy ending. While she and her immediate family escaped from Bamberg, Germany, her grandparents did not. After a long struggle to obtain visas, they were "transferred to an old age home in the East," where they perished. Rossmer was invited to return to Germany at the end of 1991 to install a sculptural ensemble that recalled her own family's emigration from Germany and the horrors of her grandparents' deportation and extermination. The exhibition took the title of *In Search of the Lost Object* and was installed in the Bamberg Municipal Museum that formerly had been the *Judenhaus*, the very place of the grandparents' house arrest.

Rossmer's installation uses artifacts that the viewer can feel, touch and read. There are photocopies of German passports and identification papers marked with a "J" (*Jude*), documents on Aryanization of the family's business and property and papers detailing the road from Germany to America, including tickets and menus from the voyage on the SS *President Harding*. Ghost-like apparitions appear amid the documents and family photographs. There are many objects, but the lost object is the one most dear that cannot be retrieved. Objects appear in a sense only as ghosts moving throughout the environment, alongside the viewer. Rossmer's individual loss becomes a tragic episode through the power of the installation, but also a metaphor for all displacement and similar suffering. What is most frightening is the conclusion that must be sensed—that this is the story of a "normal" middle-class family that suddenly found itself torn apart.

Edith Altman's father was arrested in Altenburg, Germany, and detained in Buchenwald in the days after Kristallnacht in November 1938. Eventually he was released and the family emigrated, after many desperate encounters, to Chicago. After an evolution through an academically based art, Altman became a political artist, using installations as her form of fighting racism and prejudice. Altman's chief interest is in symbols and words, which she regards as having strong positive and negative attributes. An analysis of such words and symbols and their transformation from positive to negative and back again in an alchemical manner provides a way of understanding her art and aspects of contemporary history. The Nazis, for example, used all sorts of euphemisms to describe the killing of the Jews, the ultimate one being *Endosslung* or "final solution." Other phrases and words, such as "Arbeit Macht Frei," created negative connotations to otherwise innocent words.

Altman sees her role as a priestess or shaman, with artistic powers to "reclaim" inverted symbols and words. The study of the Kabbala, with its focus on positive and negative attributes, white and black, forces of light and darkness, produces in her installation works a dialectic of words that cannot but impel the viewer to question his own values and prejudices. The Holocaust emerges as the greatest negative force. In the installation show *It was Beyond Human Imagination*, Altman asks questions about the working of the human mind and our learning processes, especially regarding definition of "the other" and victimization. The power of words is inescapable in Altman's works, as well as an understanding of how Hitler manipulated similar words as a language for genocide. Altman's healing power through art aims at deconstructing ominous symbols, like the black swastika. She changes it back to a positive force by introducing powders and earth that neutralize its negative attributes and transform it into spiritual gold. *Reclaiming the Symbol/The Art of Memory* is a powerful statement of the artist's ability to mend the world in the post-Holocaust era. Implicitly, it is the obligation of victims, like Altman herself, to take the leadership in this rebuilding process.

Gerda Meyer-Bernstein came from Hagen, Germany, to England in the 1939 children's special emigration at the age of fifteen. Later she came to Chicago. Meyer-Bernstein has been involved with the creation of politically charged installations. According to the artist, her work "is political because political events have shaped my life." Art for the artist, however, is not merely political commentary or mourning. Installation art for Meyer-Bernstein has become a way to effect nonviolent change. She has done many works on the Holocaust, as this is a direct reflection on her own life and fate, as well as that of her father, who was also an artist. However, she has also created powerful statements about other forms of violence in the twentieth century. Antiwar themes are woven into her works such as *Vietnam Memorial* (1983), *Procession* (1981) and *Garden of Eden* (1981-82). Other issues addressed in her installations include apartheid in South Africa, civil wars around the world, destruction of human lives, boat people, nuclear war and, most recently, the relationship between blacks and Jews in America. These works, when placed alongside her Holocaust installations such as *Block 11* (1989), *Volcano,* (1993) *Aus der Asch* (1985-86), *Requiem* (1983) and *Hommage of Raoul Wallenberg* (1972), suggest a redemptive role for art by opening wounds and allowing for a healing process. Meyer-Bernstein makes an important point of utilizing the Holocaust as a personal springboard for comprehending all later acts of violence. These events, however tragic they may be, are not a "Holocaust."

Meyer-Bernstein's installation for *Witness and Legacy* is *Shrine*. As an artwork, *Shrine* is an extended meditation on the meaning of Auschwitz and the people who ran it. The installation, set in a darkened room with hay strewn on the floor, evokes the bleakness of the Auschwitz environment. Barbed wires line the walls, with photographs of the crematoria and *appelplatz* (roll-call square) behind the wire. This is the world that Elie Wiesel has called "the kingdom of night," and the sense of that darkness is well understood in the darkness and silence of the installation.

The other side juxtaposes scenes of the crematoria with individual photos of Rudolph Höss, commandant at Auschwitz, who helped build the camp and run it during its first three years. Höss, who was tried in Poland after the war, came to represent the relative "normal" or banal background of perpetrators. His father wanted him to be a priest, but he often complained of the endlessness of religious ritual. Below a larger center photograph of a crematoria are three memorial candles, lit with bulbs. The overriding sense of death and hopelessness is barely relieved, except in the few photographic scenes of the outdoors. These do not necessarily suggest hope, but the other reality of deception, where the phrase "Arbeit Macht Frei" greeted inmates at the gates.

THE SECOND-GENERATION ARTISTS

Witness and Legacy contains the work of five artists who represent the second generation. Debbie Teicholz's medium is photography and photo reliefs, highly affected by use of destructive techniques of annulled images, charred wood and color tinting. Her main series, *A Prayer by the Wall,* contains strong points of reference to the Holocaust, but not in a literal manner. The evocation of images of train tracks, plowed earth, cut trees, targets and a sensitive reflection on decaying landscapes was inspired by the memory of the Holocaust on one hand and experiences in Israel. In Teicholz's photographic triptychs, the landscape of Israel and the Western Wall, the most holy site in Judaism, creates a sense of redemption, transforming the dead landscape of tracks and barren land. Teicholz's identity is strongly influenced by the memory of displacement and, being of the second generation, "My identity was greatly influenced by a past from which I am once removed. My art bears witness to this feeling of displacement, of living in a time warp, where a flashback to the Holocaust takes place simultaneously with events of today."[17] The nonspecific aspects of place suggest the difficulty of memory in identifying places of mass murder. Is this perhaps an allusion to the ethical question about how to commemorate memory in the concentration camps? Should they be left to rot and return to the earth, or should they be preserved in a fashion that might become mini-amusement parks?

Conceptually similar to the photographs of Teicholz is the work of Joyce Lyon, a Minneapolis artist whose father is a Holocaust survivor from Rzeszow, Poland. Most of his family was killed at Belzec death camp. Lyon's situation as a member of the second generation led her to inquiry about relatives who disappeared,

about literature and testimony about the Holocaust and ultimately to her own expression, *Conversations with Rzeszow: A Dialogue Exploring Different Kinds of Knowing. Conversations* is based on a series of paintings that were also transformed into a book of the same title. It is, as Lyon points out, "a dialogue between what is familiar to me…and experiences that I do not-and cannot-know first hand."[18] The artistic aspect of *Conversations* juxtaposes paintings around Rzeszow, including scenes of mass graves in the Glogow Woods, with remarkably similar landscapes from Minnesota and New York. The message is clear and suggestive of the terrible burden that memory imposes: The similarity of landscape between Poland and parts of North America indicates that memory about genocide can be induced particularly from nonpolitical sources. A bird sanctuary, woods near Tofte, Minnesota, or the remains of a razed hotel from a New York resort have a magical potency of evoking images of isolation and death in Poland's camps and forests. Just as Teicholz's enigmatic photographs of railroad tracks convey a powerful sense of tragedy, so too do Lyon's paintings suggest that the Holocaust's landscape was very much like places we know and enjoy.

Pier Marton is a second-generation artist who has wrestled with problems of his parents' survival and the impact of contemporary anti-Semitism. This led him to merge the video interview of children of survivors, called *Say I'm a Jew,* with an installation entitled *Jew,* set in a cattle car. Being a member of the second generation and experiencing European anti-Semitism in France in the 1950s and 1960s led Marton to the inability to openly express his Jewishness. Drawing from his own experience, Marton was obsessed with the question of how children of the second generation have coped with growing up in Europe after World War II. While attending a convention of second-generation survivors, Marton advertised for individuals willing to tell the story of their European and Jewish identity experiences on camera. Many volunteered. Marton edited bits and pieces of the video together to form an engaging artistic and psychological work.

The American-European painter R. J. Kitaj has represented what he terms "diasporism" as a major component in contemporary artistic life. This is a useful concept to explain the works of many artists in this show, who constantly have to deal with a Jewish identity problem in a world that is potentially enticing and supportive and also contains anti-Semitism, denial and insult. Marton's space was made to represent a blend of cattle car, barracks and a mausoleum. As Marton has written, "Memory can fuse separate locations in an inextricable blend."[19] Within the installation area were seats where the video played continuously. Those attending the show were encouraged to write their responses on the walls of the entrance and boxcar itself, recalling the memory of how deportees did the same on their way to death camps.

Mindy Weisel, a Washington-based, second-generation painter, has moved her work in the direction of an abstraction involving intensive color washes and infusion of small signs of the ever-presence of the past. This is suggestive of varying levels of emotional coping with events that were connected with her parents. Born in the Bergen-Belsen displaced persons (DP) camp in 1947, Weisel has noted that she struggled for recognition from her parents, who seemed to have established a psychic and real distance from her during childhood, a function of their own problems of survival and loss. Art for Weisel has become a method of coping with the emotions she inherited from her parents' survival. She began showing her art in 1977, and a 1980 exhibit was entitled *Paintings of the Holocaust,* a series of works done in pastel, oil paint, crayon and pencil on paper.[20] Her father's Auschwitz number figures prominently in some of the works, and most of them have a sense of brooding, although some optimism may be detected. Weisel's works have a spiritual feel to them, especially with color choice: Strong blacks, blues and aquamarine colors prevail in most of her works, often with yellowish tan backgrounds or intrusions. Symbols abound, be they concentration camp numbers, Hebrew words, or visual references. Above all, Weisel's art can be appreciated on a purely aesthetic level as abstraction, and the Holocaust-related symbols may evade the inattentive viewer.

Art Spiegelman's use of the comic book is both an innovative and problematic form of art and literary conveyance. Many survivors found *Maus* something that came close to blasphemy. The depiction of Jews as mice and Germans as cats seemed to be a somewhat unfitting reminder of German propaganda through films such as Hippler's *The Eternal Jew* (1940).

Spiegelman was the product of a thoroughly American environment of the late 1950s and 1960s, dominated by his interest in comic books and the untold story of his parents' survival. His mother, Anja, committed suicide in 1968. Subsequently, Spiegelman's father, Vladek, burned Anja's diaries. The loss of his mother as well as Anja's story was the stimulus for researching the true story of his parents' involvement in the Holocaust. The result was Art Spiegelman's more than forty hours of audio taping with Vladek Spiegelman, substantial technical and artistic research and the translating of that story into *Maus.*

Is *Maus* art? The art critic Adam Gopnik has tried to answer this interesting question:

> If you ask educated people to tell you everything they know about the history and psychology of cartooning, they will probably offer something like this: cartoons (taking caricature, political cartooning, and comic strips all together as a single form) are a relic of the infancy of art, one of the earliest forms of visual communication (and therefore, by implication, especially well-suited to children); they are naturally funny and popular; and their gift is above all for the diminutive.[21]

Gopnik goes on to suggest the truth is actually the opposite and that cartoons represent "a relatively novel offspring of an extremely sophisticated visual culture."[22]

Previous exhibitions of Spiegelman's drawings have made it clear that he first utilized the format of *Maus* in *Prisoner on the Hell Planet* in 1972. His first idea for the mouse metaphor was to apply it to the history of African Americans, but he soon applied it to the Jews. As Spiegelman progressed into the drawing of *Maus,* he became concerned with various aesthetic aspects that were important from the point of view of the visual artist. "He was becoming increasingly concerned with deconstructing the basic narrative and visual elements of the comic strip: How does one panel on a page relate to others? How do a strip's artificial cropping and use of pictorial illusion manipulate reality?…How do words and pictures combine in the human brain."[23] In this quest, the artist rejected photo-realism, elaborate detailing and shading, and ultimately developed a particular reduction process in which text was reduced to fit the artistic space.

Witness and Legacy marks a beginning of the process of investigating the subject of the Holocaust. In addition, the exhibition raises the greater question of whether or not it is possible to enter into the subject without trivializing the event and developing visual forms that are distortions. Just as Greek and Roman art developed their own symbols based on mythology and Christian art symbols relate to the Passion of Jesus and the biblical stories, so too is a common visual language emerging to describe the Holocaust. In this Holocaust imagery, there is a spectrum that runs from the realistic scenes of barbed wire, gas chambers, crematoria, children, mounds of bodies and relics to more abstract, metaphorical and allusive gestures.

From the perspective of the Torah, the Holocaust demands some reinvestigation of old stories and their current meaning: the presence of God, original sin, the sacrifice of Isaac, the story of Job. Beyond this is the story of man himself, with both the potential for good and evil. Christian and Jewish theologians have both asked the questions: "Where was man?" and "Where was God?"

As the twentieth century closes, there is more and more of a burden and an increasing urgency to tell the story. The generation of witnesses is passing. All that will be left is the legacy. Throughout history, art has been a means of such telling. Within the realm of art, the Holocaust era may just be emerging.

Stephen C. Feinstein
Co-curator of *Witness and Legacy*
University of Wisconsin at River Falls

NOTES

1. Elie Wiesel, "Art and the Holocaust: Trivializing Memory," *New York Times,* Sunday, 11 June 1989, sec. 2.

2. The literature on the destruction of the Gypsies is complicated by negative stereotypes both before and after World War II, lack of literary tradition among the Romani and Sinti peoples, absence of significant numbers of both memoirs and scholarly books and few representative artists. The only Gypsy artist who has been exhibited recently is Karl Stojko, who survived Auschwitz and lives in Austria.

3. Raul Hilberg, *Perpetrators, Victims, Bystanders* (New York: HarperCollins, 1992), 11.

4. James T. Young, *Writing and Rewriting the Holocaust* (Bloomington: Indiana University Press, 1988), 96-97.

5. Leonard Baskin, *Iconologia* (London: Harcourt, Brace and Jovanovich, 1988), 22.

6. Ibid., 23.

7. Wiesel, "Art and the Holocaust."

8. Frank Rich, "The Holocaust Boom," *New York Times,* 7 April 1994, A15.

9. Raul Hilberg, "Conscience from Burlington," *Hadassah Magazine,* August/September 1991, 23.

10. Primo Levi as quoted in Michael Kimmelman, "Horror Unforgotten: The Politics of Memory," *New York Times,* Friday, 11 March 1994, B1.

11. Wiesel, "Art and the Holocaust."

12. Paul Richard, "Obscene Pleasure: Art Among the Corpses," *Washington Post,* Sunday, 18 April 1993, G6.

13. Ken Johnson, "Art and Memory," *Art in America,* November 1993, 98.

14. For purposes of the exhibition, "American" was defined as artists currently living and working in the United States.

15. "Minutes of the Exhibition Jury, March 16, 1943, Vilna Ghetto." Translation of YIVO Document #466 by Dina Abramowicz. (New York: YIVO Institute for Jewish Research).

16. Samuel Bak as quoted in *Bak: Oils, Watercolors, Drawings, 1972-1974* (New York: Aberbach Fine Art, October-November 1974), 3.

17. Paul Kresh, "Photograph Exhibit Evokes Memories of the Holocaust," *Jewish Weeks, Inc.,* May 10-16, 1991, 38.

18. Joyce Lyon, *Conversations with Rzezsow* (Minneapolis: Wallace Carlson Co., 1993).

19. Pier Marton, letter to Stephen Feinstein, 11 April 1994.

20. For an extended discussion of Weisel's background with longer personal statements, see Vivian Alpert Thompson, *A Mission in Art* (Macon, Ga.: Mercer University Press, 1988), 94-95. Weisel's mother died in 1994.

21. Adam Gopnik, "Comics and Catastrophe," *New Republic,* 22 June 1987.

22. Ibid.

23. Galerie St. Etienne, *Art Spiegelman: The Road to Maus* (New York: Galerie St. Etienne, 1992). Exhibition brochure.

AND THE LION SHALL DWELL WITH THE FISH

The Holocaust Experience as Reflected by Five Installation Artists

The plant sprouting from this dream ladder of mine, had a fascinating and utterly beautiful shape....One of the most astonishing fruits I ever encountered on this plant, was my old friend the fish....I first met the fish in my childhood. Every Jewish kid had a chance to eat fish, but this fish of mine was not intended for eating. My father was swinging it above our heads in one hand, while mumbling a silent prayer. The traditional fowl used for expiatory sacrifice was disqualified that year, during those fearful days, in fear its crow would turn us in. So the fish took its place. The fish is a silent victim. It can't cry out against oppression. This fish is so close to me that if it miraculously grew on me—like a hand, I would accept it as a natural anatomic growth. In absolute contrast to it, as far as I am concerned, stands the lion. The living, mourning lion, standing on his slaughtered kin's grave. The bereaved lion is weeping, for he was doomed to be the sole survivor, and the keeper of his people's glowing ember....The fact that I lived through this, puts a responsibility on me: It commands me to testify as to what happened, and if only by way of my humble means: line and color.[1]

—*Naftali Bezem, 1972*

At the age of fourteen, in August 1939, Naftali Bezem arrived in Palestine alone. He did not understand why his parents had boarded him on a train bound for this strange, remote and desolate place. Little did he know he would never see them again. Thirty years later, a prominent Israeli artist, he still empathized with the fish—he was not taught to cry foul. But destiny had left him with a legacy, and he had been transformed into the weeping lion, whose roar was to be heard to the edge of the earth. And the lion shall dwell with the fish forever in his soul. Robert J. Lifton, reflecting on this sense of destiny, has suggested that "the impulse to bear witness, beginning with a sense of responsibility to the dead, can readily extend into a 'survivor mission.'"[2]

Although the five installation artists presented in our exhibition are not survivors in the traditional sense of the word, the four born in Europe had firsthand experiences regarding the events of the Holocaust—events that eventually shaped their future. When approached to comment on the rationale behind creating these works, they reiterated the "survivor mission." The fish, as a comforting and inviting option for the process of healing personal and private wounds, posed no viable choice. The legacy called for "the lion's roar"—the individual tragedy was enlisted to a higher cause. The responsibility is to remember—for everyone to remember.

When analyzing the installations displayed in *Witness and Legacy*, one can see the close ties between the personal histories of the artists and their creations. Meaningful childhood experiences, mainly those that pose conflicts, had a direct impact on their art. At times the four survivor or second-generation artists among the five feel that relatives who never made it to American shores were uninvited ghosts, occupying a residency in their own childhood memories. Later in life, they comprehended that these family members lost in the Holocaust never ceased to be part of their parents' existence. By way of transfusion and by identification, the parents transferred their own sense of pain and loss to their children and bestowed upon them the legacy of becoming a living *yahrzeit* (memorial candle). As Gabrielle Rossmer has commented: "What I always knew, though, was the intense pain that my father felt over losing his parents. I became aware that the great sadness that my father felt was something I actually felt as well."[3]

EDITH ALTMAN

> It is important to preserve these memories, not only to memorialize those who died, but also, to remember that it actually happened. These memories carry with them a responsibility, I would say.[4]

> The artist doesn't always choose her subjects. Sometimes the time and place in history demands that certain work be done.[5]

Edith Altman was born in Altenburg, Germany. She was eight years old on Kristallnacht, November 9, 1938, when German troops came to the family home and took her father to one of many subsequent detentions in the nearby Buchenwald concentration camp. Altman's father fled to the United States in May 1939 by obtaining a forged passport. For the family left behind, conditions worsened. She and her brother were expelled from school and the family's property was confiscated. As conditions deteriorated, Altman's mother fled with the children to Amsterdam and later to the United States to reunite with her husband. When the war was over, it was learned that all eight of his siblings had perished in concentration camps.

After her father's death, Altman was compelled to return to the place where he was made victim. "I hoped that if I was able to reevaluate fears of old anger I could achieve balance in my life. My father's acceptance of his role as victim was his torment, and he could not help but turn his torment against those he loved." The shamanlike ritual Altman performed in Buchenwald in 1984 was her attempt to cleanse herself from this *dibbuk* (demon). This act enabled her, forty-five years after she had escaped Germany, to unite opposites: pain and joy, good and evil, anger and forgiveness.

In her installation *The Art of Memory: Reclaiming the Symbol,* Altman throws the spectator into the shaman's chamber. On one wall we are faced with a dominant, giant, gold swastika, with its mirror image, now in the familiar black Nazi color, rested on the floor. The wall on the opposite end of the room has detached elements of the Star of David, a shape made of triangles,

used in different colors by the Nazis to identify other groups of prisoners: Communists, Gypsies and homosexuals. Incorporating textual and visual elements as didactic material to study these images, Altman encourages the onlooker to redefine his relationships with these symbols, so heavily burdened by attributes, evil or good, assigned by past societies and cultures. In her shaman dance, Altman has made gold out of base matter. Now she assumes the role of the alchemist, and we take part in her transformation of nature—in this case the nature of symbols.

GABRIELLE ROSSMER

Rossmer was born in Bamberg, Germany. By 1933 the thriving Jewish community of one thousand people dwindled to a few elderly souls. During the previous decade, only ten Jewish children were born in the city, Gabrielle being one of them. The morning after Kristallnacht, along with all Jewish males under the age of sixty-five, Rossmer's father was arrested and sent to Dachau concentration camp. After five weeks he returned home. Soon after, the parents, with one-year-old Gabrielle, boarded the SS *President Harding* in Hamburg, bound for New York.

Left behind were Rossmer's grandparents, as well as an aunt and uncle. New rules and decrees restricted their lives. Gradually they lost all their possessions and civil rights. In a letter of July 1941, written to their son Stephen in New York, the grandfather urged him to act fast on the immigration forms from Washington. Unfortunately, Rossmer's grandparents never made it to America. They were deported in the Spring of 1942 and perished in Poland, east of Lublin. By November 1942, all the Jews of Bamberg were gone.

Stephen Rossmer, Gabrielle's father, died in 1983. At the funeral, she read a poem he had written for her as a child. Its last stanza reads:

> Grandparents who never came
> A sacrifice to Germany's shame
> We will always remember you
> We are tied to you
> by an eternal bond.[6]

After the funeral, Rossmer observed that "there I discovered the bond that he has left me as a legacy."[7] The result was the exhibition at Hainstrasse 4a in Bamberg, which Rossmer described as "truly a site specific piece of work....But I don't feel that I have finished the task of re-shaping memory, and examining history, and memorializing those we have lost."[8]

In her installation *In Search of the Lost Object,* we find the most direct encounter with ghost imagery: the suspended freestanding figures made of stiffened gauze—hollow shells, faceless and bodiless. Rossmer recounted her experience mounting the installation in Bamberg, which by the strangest coincidence took place in the city's Municipal Museum, where in 1943 her grand-parents resided before their deportation. Ross-mer refers to the space as "the place where the ghosts of my grandparents also resided."[9] A closer look at the seemingly classical drapery, reminiscent of the famous female figures of Ec-clesia and Synagoga in the Gothic cathedral of the city, reveals it is soiled by ashes. The eter-nally blindfolded Synagoga is mourning for the dead.

Holocaust ghosts haunt one's life not only as embodiments of lost family members. They transform to feelings of hate and anger: "My fa-ther lived the rest of his life angry. He trusted no one. He never resolved the torment of being the one who survived."[10]

GERDA MEYER-BERNSTEIN

> In my native Germany, I witnessed severe vi-olence and social upheaval and was perma-nently marked by it. I made a vow not to remain silent.[11]

Gerda Meyer-Bernstein was born in Westphalia, Germany, and spent the larger part of her child-hood in Nazi Germany. On Kristallnacht, Novem-ber 9, 1938, fifteen-year-old Gerda, with her family, had to hide on the roof of their home. While her immediate family eventually managed to leave Germany for London and subsequently Amer-ica, her grandmother, aunt and uncles did not.

Although Gerda Meyer-Bernstein fled her na-tive Germany like Altman and Rossmer, she does not reflect on personal demons haunting her memory. What she remembers most is po-litical injustice, a theme that can be understood in terms of the linkage she establishes between the Holocaust and the current American social agenda. "My work is political because political events have shaped my life. The political and so-cial upheaval I witnessed in my native Germany has sensitized me to all political atrocities. My concerns are racism, sexism, censorship, politi-cal killings....Man's inhumanity to man."[12]

Meyer-Bernstein's installation *Shrine* is but one in a series of works that were shaped by her political conscience. Her art becomes a weapon in fighting for the elimination of extreme horrors and violence, be they in Hiroshima or South Africa. Like other contemporary American artists, she reflects on the beastly aspects of the twen-tieth century as it comes to a close. For Meyer-Bernstein, the Holocaust experience bears one important lesson—silence leads to consent. Her art is a nonviolent revolution, as it constitutes the means of effecting change. *Shrine*—a black, painted chamber with barbed wire and a series of images of the crematoria at Auschwitz inter-cepted by images of the appelplatz—recalls the doom and the hope of the inmates in the con-centration camps. Photographs of the ultimate destruction site of the Holocaust and pho-tographs of its commandant, Rudolph Höss, at his postwar trial in Poland enable the viewer to make an intellectual linkage with the historical events of the past, while the grim, dimly lit en-vironment evokes an emotional response. Meyer-Bernstein hopes that by experiencing this cohesive whole, her audience will pose the inevitable question: "Why is there so much violence?"[13]

PIER MARTON

> The prophet Joel said tell your children about the exodus. Here we are a generation after the Holocaust and it is unbelievable as the waters parting! My parents' generation will slowly disappear, but the energy that created the Holocaust is still there. To forget is to kill twice.[14]

Pier Marton was born in France. His father was in the French Resistance. Being an artist and photographer, he forged documents and helped hide German deserters, actions for which he was almost shot by the German Gestapo. At the same time, Marton's mother was hiding in Hun-gary, in the back room of a commandant's office, sharing the space with eight other people, in-cluding a baby.

Marton grew up in a Parisian apartment building that contained active memories of the Holocaust years in France. Years before, his father had created an escape route in the same apartment by sawing through an iron grill, which could be removed quickly. The presence of an escape route served as a constant reminder to Marton that one had to have fast legs to stay alive—legs his great grandfather and grandmother did not have. They perished in Auschwitz.

After his father's death, Marton left France for America. For him, living in France was like living in a place where one needs constantly to know the route for escape. That claustrophobic cloud prompted his departure from France, where Marton felt he was surrounded by the same people who had betrayed his grandmother. Marton recognized the direct linkage of his family annals to his artistic oeuvre: "Knowing our parents had almost been killed many times, we grew up with a particular chill in our bones…in our homes and elsewhere, our families' grief, terror and anger found very little room to heal. I am a witness to my parents, their wound is mine."[15]

However, unlike Altman and Rossmer, Marton elected to escape from European soil, where the Holocaust occurred. He carried with him his Jewishness as a badge of shame, and only in his new world could he free himself from his haunting ghost—the shame of being Jewish. Thus, in Marton's installation *Jew,* which includes a powerful, short documentary film *Say I'm a Jew,* the viewer is immersed into the artist's search for Jewish identity among the second generation. Seated on wooden benches in a simulated railroad cattle car, the viewer sees a video of collaged interviews with men and women who, like Marton, are children of European survivors now living in the United States. Those who speak on Marton's video describe their struggle of carrying the legacy and their rejection and acceptance of their Jewish heritage. The chorus of different voices says things that are hard to say and hard to hear. For Marton, to say the unspeakable is the only process for liberation—"to communicate one's own inhibitions, own oneself, the positive and negative, neglecting neither."[16] The purpose of the exhibit for Marton does not end with self-healing, nor is it about creating guilt. It is about "what we can do to fight racism and anti-Semitism."[17]

This last remark by Marton brings to surface the complexity of second-generation issues and the fact that the artist's inner realm is not limited to his personal memories. In fact, artists like Marton simultaneously wish to express the collective memory, the subconsciousness of the human race, from a Jewish perspective. This underlying universal moral objective is the backbone of all the installations in this exhibition. The stimulus in each case was a personal, firsthand experience. Gabrielle Rossmer's *In Search of the Lost Object* is the story of one Bamberg Jewish family. The faded family photographs, along with records, documents and letters, attest to the normal life before the upheaval and serve as a means to attain an intimate look at the family's saga. However, Bamberg is nothing less than Germany, and the Rossmers' story is the story of the six million—the story of racial persecution fifty years ago in Nazi Germany. If the Holocaust is incomprehensible to the human mind, the Rossmers' escape and partial destruction, like Spielberg's *Schindler's List,* is a story we can follow and internalize, and thus it can serve as a lesson for generations to come. In *Kunst Arbeit,* the catalog that accompanied Edith Altman's installation *Reclaiming the Symbol* in Chicago, the artist noted that "I seek to take my work to a more transcendental level…to consider social issues. My art, I hope, becomes a vehicle for contemplation about humanity."[18]

Contemplation does not suffice for Altman. In the same interview she specifically mentions *Tikkun Olam,* a Jewish Kabbalistic notion that we can take an active part in the process of repair, the betterment of the world. By posing an ethical challenge for her installation, Altman implies the intrinsic quality of her work to instigate change—here and now. "The installation can only have a meaning if we get actively involved.…It questions whether we are moved to take any kind of action when faced with evidence of others' pain."[19]

PEARL HIRSHFIELD

Pearl Hirshfield, is the only installation artist in the *Witness and Legacy* exhibition who was born in America. Her family, of Russian-Jewish background, arrived before the events of the Holocaust. As a Chicago native, she represents the American humanist conscience. A quick glance at her extensive past political actions reveals her involvement, both as artist and as political activist, on issues pertaining to the peace movement, nuclear disarmament, fighting racism and supporting rights for women. As she has articulated in a personal statement, "My art centers on the outrage I feel when confronted with the inequities and injustices of society, whether local, national or global." Because of her world-encompassing view, Hirshfield expresses her personal linkage to the events of the Holocaust as she continues: "I have been to Auschwitz-Birkenau...to find any trace of relatives who perished....It has been an ongoing painful and difficult process."[20] The same trip took Hirshfield to Hiroshima and Nagasaki, where she tried to make personal connections with the survivors of this disaster of war. Reflecting on both, Hirshfield admits that she still continues to attempt to make sense out of these two events in her work.

At the entrance to *Shadows of Auschwitz,* her current installation, Hirshfield places a quote by Primo Levi: "Beyond the fence stand the lords of death, and not far away the train is awaiting...." This sets the physical and emotional mood of the installation space. The spectator is drawn into a darkened interior space, where the artist makes use of an array of vertical mirrors to effect dramatic changes in light and shadow, with light piercing through horizontal slots. The "height" of the experience awaits the viewer at the other side of the fence, where he encounters his own reflection with numbers across his body. The numbers are the actual Auschwitz numbers of survivors Hirshfield has met. They are authentic. Invention is not needed in this environment. An exit sign marked *Ausgang* directs one to the outside, but leaving with mentally tattooed numbers. Where does it lead to? Hirshfield would like to hope that we will all join the ranks of those protesting injustice, inhumanity, and persecution of every color or shape on the face of our globe.

Thus far, the main issues articulated have focused on what these five installation artists wished to address in their works and the reasons they ventured into this highly charged subject matter. However, the question remains why so many artists in this show have chosen installation as their medium. Although there have been many predecessors in the form of assemblage,

environmental art and happenings from previous decades, the eighties with their turbulence and violence have instigated a flourishing of site-specific installations.

In many ways installation art represents an integral segment of the larger trend toward recognizable imagery, sometimes called "New Imagism." Artists in this group share an emphasis on narrative and content. They attempt to build a stronger bond between the art world and the so-called "real world" of social change. In this larger realm of New Imagism, artists like Borofsky, Bosman and Golub feel a need to direct their art toward specific aspects of their cultural, social or personal agenda. In this manner, their art is a manifestation of a certain social climate. The eighties expressed a heightened anxiety regarding the gloomy end of the twentieth century, which offers only a dark apocalyptic vision of the future. Thus, art needs to communicate these fears more directly, in the hope that the course of doom will change. As different types of social violence are expressed, however, most artists resort to the use of archival media, images, photographs, video and television clips to achieve the desired resonance between art and reality.

These artists do not echo the others, but are equal voices that work in unison. Artists now confront head-on the interactive role of art in society. As the artist attempts to challenge the viewer, to force him into participation, installation art offers a viable solution. The signs *Eingang* (Entrance) and *Ausgang* (Exit) in Hirshfield's installation, for example, are a tangible reminder that we enter a space, just as we do a theater. Now we are totally immersed in the artist's reality, where we are not allowed a passive role. The viewer is challenged to reconsider old premises he has brought along. He is bombarded with static visual images, textual information, moving images and sound. This is not a time to contemplate a single element in this reconstructed reality. The viewer is challenged to absorb the complexities of this alternative environment as a whole. Intellectual and expressive modes are utilized to enhance new association, new perception by the viewer. Now the artist waits to see what course his changed citizen of the world will take: silent as the fish or active as the lion.

Edith Altman, Gerda Meyer-Bernstein, Pearl Hirshfield, Pier Marton and Gabrielle Rossmer, by opting to use installations as the medium for their art, join the ranks of American artists of the eighties and nineties who wish to escape the "commodification" of art in the galleries. They are artists who rejected art for art's sake and enlisted themselves and their art to projects with social and moral accountability and responsibility. They are artists who are committed to making a change, yet maintain a fine edge in their aesthetics.

In the beginning there was silence. The Holocaust wasn't discussed too much and wasn't taught. Its manifestations were found occasionally in art, literature and film. Suddenly, in the eighties, there was a sense of urgency for Jews to make themselves heard, to make themselves understood. Survivors will die and no direct witnesses will be able to bear witness. Following the initial repression, when we all embraced Bezem's fish mentality, a subsequent energized release of memory in all forms took place. Holocaust museums grew with public support in Washington and Los Angeles. Millions filled theaters to see *Schindler's List. Witness and Legacy* is but one more manifestation of the imprint of the Holocaust on human consciousness and on art in particular. Yet the exhibition bears the responsibility to join the lion's roar.

Yehudit Shendar
Classical and Near Eastern Studies Department
University of Minnesota

NOTES

1. Naftali Bezem, *Boats, Immigrants, Parents and Cabinets, Tables and Chairs, Blessing the Candles, Lions and Fish, Plants* (Ramat Gan: Masada, 1972), 14.

2. Robert Jay Lifton, "Witnessing Survival," *Society* 15 (March/April 1978): 43.

3. Gabrielle Rossmer, artist statement (unpublished, typed manuscript), 3.

4. Mary Jane Jacob, "The Artist in Society," *Kunst Arbeit* (Chicago: State of Illinois Art Gallery, 1992), 2.

5. Rochelle Segal, "On Exhibit: A Jewish Artist Confronts the Swastika," *Reader,* 26 Nov. 1993.

6. Gabrielle Rossmer, *In Search of the Lost Object* (Boston: The Space, 1993).

7. Ibid.

8. Rossmer, artist statement.

9. Rossmer, *In Search of the Lost Object,* 4.

10. Gabrielle Rossmer, artist statement (unpublished, typed manuscript), 1992. Unpaginated.

11. Gerda Meyer-Bernstein, artist statement, *Gerda Meyer-Bernstein* (Chicago: Beacon Street Gallery, 1993), 7.

12. Ibid.

13. Gerda Meyer-Bernstein, *Political Visions: Installation und Objekten* (Berlin: Neuer Berliner Kunsverein, 1987).

14 Karen Boren Swedin, "To Forget the Past is to Kill Twice," *Today,* 5 April 1991.

15. Pier Marton, artist statement, *JEW* (Chicago: Spertus Museum, 1990).

16. Gary Reynolds, "Public Secrets/Private Revelations," *Changing Channels* (Minneapolis: UC Video, May 1985), 6.

17. Mary Jane Jacob, *Artist in Society,* 4.

18. Ibid., 5.

19. Edith Altman, artist statement, *Exodus Repair,* (Akademie Der Kunste Berlin, 1986).

20. Pearl Hirshfield, unpublished artist statement.

THE PERSISTENCE OF HOLOCAUST IMAGERY IN AMERICAN ART

Today, fifty years after the end of World War II, more American artists than ever before are using Holocaust imagery. The artists include concentration camp survivors, others who experienced Nazi brutality directly and those who were born in the United States and elsewhere both before and after the war. Although each artist works in his or her own particular way, their art is not differentiated by age, experience or personal memory. What they do share are greater or lesser amounts of anger, desire for reconciliation of people, the necessity of remembrance and a concern for victims of brutality in Vietnam, Bosnia and elsewhere. But in most instances, the spark that ignites this aspect of their art is the Holocaust.

Of the many artists who use such imagery, I want to discuss only a handful whose work has been available to the public through gallery and museum exhibitions and installations. Compared to American artists who used Holocaust imagery in the 1940s, 1950s and 1960s, contemporary figures are distinguished by two characteristics. First, they are more interested in Jewish particularity than in universalizing their subject matter to include the sufferings and afflictions of others. It is as if they instinctively understand literary historian Alvin Rosenfeld's admonition that "to generalize or universalize the victims of the Holocaust is not only to profane their memories but to exonerate their executioners."[1] And second, there is little interest in couching their imagery in mythological or biblical imagery derived from sources such as Lamentations or the Book of Job.

A few examples may be given at first from artists who do not appear in *Witness and Legacy,* not because of artistic quality but simply because of space considerations. Murray Zimiles

(born in the United States) ignores myth because "the subject requires force, not myth." Zimiles, who paints burning Polish synagogues, goes on to say that "the artist must confront the viewer in an unambiguous way. He must show the horror, the pain and the loss. The image must be a vehicle that propels the viewer into a world of undeniable recognition of what happened fifty years ago."[2] Howard Lee Theile (born in the United States) also finds less need for mythological or biblical imagery because "right here on earth the Germans made manifest for us what massive, unrelenting, inescapable suffering and despair looked like. For me," Theile says, "any introduction of myth or drama can only serve to reduce the horrible reality of the Holocaust."[3] American-born Marty Kalb finds the public less knowledgeable about biblical sources and therefore cannot make appropriate connections between such imagery and the Holocaust. Rather, he believes that "a direct graphic representation of an incident can usually transcend the barrier to communication."[4]

Gerda Meyer-Bernstein (born in Germany), whose installation *Shrine* appears in *Witness and Legacy,* witnessed Kristallnacht and states simply that documenting the Holocaust is more important now than ever before. We have an obligation and a responsibility to "re-examine and analyze the atrocities of the Holocaust." She wants people to deal directly with their feelings and attitudes, and, as the Holocaust recedes into memory, she wants her art to be more confrontational, as if to deny the passage of time. To make her points with clarity, she has exhibited *Block 11* in dark, claustrophobic spaces since 1982. It is made up of about 550 suitcases covered with names, birth dates and concentration camp numbers of both the living and dead. She feels that in such environments there is little chance to escape direct confrontation with these suitcases and what they represent.[5]

Pearl Hirshfield (born in the United States) has also created spaces that evoke concentration camp experiences by creating installations resembling cattle cars and ramps. In *Shadows of Auschwitz,* originally exhibited in 1986 and reproduced for *Witness and Legacy,* she includes a part of a cattle car and a section that includes mirrors with numbers painted on them, so that the viewer sees him or herself reflected with a number across the body. In *Shadow of Birkenau-Zur Desinfektion* of 1993, the viewer enters a narrow corridor bounded by fences and paintings to suggest brick chimneys. There are naked electric lightbulbs and photos of victims collaged to various surfaces. The exit corridor, lit by a red light, contains a mirror to which is attached a sign: *Zur Desinfektion.*[6]

It is as if in these works the artists are recalling visually what novelist Cynthia Ozick suggested verbally: "The task is to retrieve the Holocaust freight car by freight car, tower by tower, road by road, document by document. *The task is to save it from becoming literature.*"[7] These artists, in their different ways, are saving the Holocaust from becoming art, preferring instead to emphasize, obviously from a distance, the look and feel of the camps.

Pier Marton (born in France after the war) also used a simulated cattle car for one of his video pieces entitled *Say I'm A Jew,* first seen in 1985. The piece lasts twenty-eight minutes. From benches viewers watch a video screen on which European-born Jews now living in the United States discuss anti-Semitic incidents experienced in Europe. Works of this sort serve as historical reminders of European anti-Semitism as well as help exorcise those experiences by allowing the participants to talk about their feelings. But such memories can be so traumatic that one of the first times Marton had to say "I am a Jew" before a group of people he almost fainted, so overwhelming were his anxiety and fear.[8]

Many American-born Jews, in search of an ancestral home, have enshrined the shtetls and ghettos of Eastern Europe with a bittersweet nostalgia based on family reminiscences, novels and short stories. American-born Eleanor Antin, who in 1992 produced a silent, black-and-white film *The Man Without a World,* has said, "What haunts me is the loss of the rich Jewish culture of Eastern Europe, the world the Holocaust destroyed. That loss, and the need to invoke it, are at the core of my Jewish works."[9] *The Man Without a World,* starring Pier Marton, evokes the lost world of the shtetl. And in 1994, Antin completed an installation in the Jewish Museum of New York called *Vilna Nights,* in which the viewer looks into a courtyard partially destroyed by bombs. In the windows, the viewer sees aspects of Jewish life projected by video discs.

The shtetl also appears in the works of Ruth Weisberg and Murray Zimiles. Weisberg's 1971 book, *The Shtetl: A Journey and a Memorial,* includes imagined views of shtetl life, based on the supposition that the artist "might have been amongst them" and that she is now "a branch, a resting place for their souls."[10] Zimiles, on the other hand, has depicted scenes of destruction of synagogues in his *Fire Paintings* of 1994. For Zimiles, the burning of these great synagogues marked the end of Jewish culture itself in Poland.[11] Discussing the motivation for these works Zimiles has said, no doubt reflecting the thoughts of many, that "the Holocaust is the pivotal event of our century and perhaps of all human history. As an artist it is my obligation to deal with this subject."

For Howard Lee Theile, who has painted portraits of camp survivors from archival photographs, the question is not why an artist should employ Holocaust imagery, but rather how to find the most effective kind of presentation in order to make impossible the act of forgetting. Jerome Witkin, born in the United States in 1939, finds that the Holocaust did not exist only from 1933 to 1945, but rather "in every moment from that time onwards forever." He has asked, "how can an imagist not paint this and not become obsessed by it?" So strong are his feelings that he has called his paintings of Holocaust scenes "my purpose in life."[12] Of all the works by artists in America, his are the most nightmarish. One three-part work completed in 1981, *Death as an Usher: Berlin 1933,* includes a theater interior, a Hitler-like usher who lights the way to the exit of death, and the victim, a young girl who runs toward her doom or toward the final solution. Another multipart work, *The Butcher's Helpers* of 1992, depicts the sadistic mutilation of helpless victims.[13] Witkin's contribution to *Witness and Legacy* is *The Beating Station, Berlin, 1933,* which shows the brutality of Nazi rape and street violence.

By contrast, two artists who experienced brutality firsthand have painted works much more muted in their effects. Alice Lok Cahana, who was an inmate at Auschwitz and liberated at Bergen-Belsen, refuses to reveal the kind of anger of Zimiles and Witkin. She has said that if she hates, then she has been contaminated by Hitler's germs and that she will not pass on that kind of hate. Yet for her there is the necessity to tell the stories she has witnessed, even if there is no language to describe the horrendous experiences. So, her images are semi-abstracted and often veiled behind washes of beautiful color.[14] Hannelore Baron, a survivor who died in 1987, made small assemblages of paper and wood that suggest time's ravages and, more important, secrets hidden behind closed and boarded-up spaces. For many camp survivors and children hidden during the war, such as those found in the paintings of Kitty Klaidman, allusion substitutes for description, whether in conversation or in art, of the memories too horrendous to confront directly, let alone reveal to the public.

But what about imagery that suggests the inability to cope with or respond to the brutalization inflicted upon Jews, imagery that suggests that there is no meaning in suffering and death, imagery visually equivalent to these words written by literary historian Alvin Rosenfeld: "There are no metaphors for Auschwitz, just as Auschwitz is not a metaphor for anything else. The flames were real flames, the ashes only ashes, the smoke always only smoke. [The burnings] can only be or mean what they in fact were: the death of the Jews."[15] The work of Israeli-born Natan Nuchi (who is not represented in this exhibition) visually parallels these remarks more than the works of other artists with whom I am familiar. His emaciated nudes, which float in a nonenvironment, seem stripped of everything. They seem to be neither survivors nor victims, but rather products of moral meaninglessness, of societal nothingness and universal indifference. They seem neither dead nor alive, but totally dehumanized. Nuchi's figures also seem to be the sad embodiment of critic Andreas Huyssen's words: "After we have remembered, gone through the facts, mourned the victims, we will still be haunted by that core of absolute humiliation, degradation, and horror suffered by the victims."[16]

In contrast, Edith Altman, who experienced Kristallnacht as a child, has developed imagery that is both interactive and mystical. Her first piece with Jewish subject matter, dating from 1987, is called *When We Are Born, We Are Given a Golden Tent, and All of Life is the Folding and Unfolding of the Tent.* The work includes a gold-painted canvas tent with images of herself and her father, who was briefly imprisoned after Kristallnacht. Altman has carried the tent to various parts of Europe and America and has invited people into the tent to speak about, as she says, "the pain of the past that we shared." Altman says that she wants to draw God's presence into the tent for purposes of healing and transformation, for the sense of *Tikkun Olam* (To mend the world). The tent is not a fixed structure, but rather symbolic of constructing temples within ourselves to house spiritual presences during our wanderings through life. As Altman says, "I was trying to face a personal dark as well as the darkness felt by other people."[17]

For Jews, the swastika, of course, is one of the darkest images to contemplate. Altman incorporates it into the multimedia installation of 1992, repeated in *Witness and Legacy,* called *Reclaiming the Symbol/The Art of Memory.* She used it for two main reasons. First, she wanted to overcome the sense of fear it created. Second, she hoped to restore its ancient meaning as a symbol of revival and prosperity. She said, "By taking the swastika apart, by deconstructing its meaning and disempowering it, I hoped to change its fearful energy. In a spiritual and mystical kind of way, I am exorcising its evil memory in hopes of healing our fear."[18] In this regard, her response is one of triumphant counter-aggression—to take a symbol that was perverted by the Nazis and restore it to its original meaning, to wipe out the memory of its use by the Nazis. This work is the only Holocaust-inspired work I know of that dwells on Jewish response rather than Jewish victimization. As such, it is as rare as its concept is interesting.

All of these artists are involved, as historian Lucy Dawidowicz has stated, in a "secular act of bearing witness to Auschwitz and the mystery of Jewish survival."[19] But serious questions must be raised about these works and what they might represent, particularly in the United States where so many Jews have been acculturated if not totally assimilated. Does remembering the Holocaust substitute for a live ethnic culture? Does remembering the Holocaust substitute for some distinctive everyday practice? Do these works contribute to the substitution of a Holocaust memory for active participation in Jewish life? As Pier Marton, the author of the video *Say I'm a Jew,* has said, "As a non-religious Jew, you have only a tradition of martyrdom. I don't say that one needs to become religious. But to look at this huge body of Jewish knowledge and not to do your best to pass it on, to honor it, is another type of murder. It is my responsibility to know as much as I can."[20] For Jews, the value of all of these works, then, must lie not just in memorializing the most tragic episode in Jewish history, but in helping forge a modern Jewish identity.

Matthew Baigell
Professor of Art History
Rutgers University
New Brunswick, New Jersey

NOTES

1. Alvin Rosenfeld, *A Double Dying: Reflections on Holocaust Literature* (Bloomington: Indiana University Press, 1980), 160.

2. Personal correspondence, March 17, 1994.

3. Personal correspondence, February 3, 1994.

4. Personal correspondence, March 18, 1994.

5. Personal correspondence, March 24, 1994; and *Present at the Creation* (Chicago: Chicago Public Library Cultural Center, 1989), 26-27.

6. Personal correspondence, May 30, 1992; and Tarara Siuda, "Art Exhibit Recalls Auschwitz," *Mundelein [College] Scholar,* 6 (November 17, 1989): 1.

7. Cynthia Ozick, "The Uses of Legend: Elie Wiesel as Tsaddik," *Congress Bi-Weekly* (June 9, 1969): 19, cited in Alan L. Berger, *Crisis and Covenant: The Covenant in American Jewish Fiction* (Albany: State University of New York Press, 1985), 194.

8. Personal correspondence, May 21, 1992.

9. Personal correspondence, April 4, 1994.

10. Ruth Weisberg, *The Shtetl: A Journey and a Memorial* (The Kelyn Press, 1971). Weisberg's statement has been recorded at various times. See, for instance, Ora Lerman, "Autobiographical Journey: Can Art Transform Personal and Cultural Loss?" *Arts Magazine,* May 1985, 103.

11. Personal correspondence, March 1, 1994; and Murray Zimiles: *The Fire Paintings, The Book of Fire* (New York: Stuart Levy Gallery, 1993).

12. Personal correspondence, December 12, 1992, and March 3, 1994.

13. Sherry Chayat, *Life Lessons: The Art of Jerome Witkin* (Syracuse: Syracuse University Press, 1994), plate 6.

14. *From Ashes to the Rainbow: A Tribute to Raoul Wallenburg. Works by Alice Lok Cahana* (Los Angeles: Hebrew Union College Skirball Museum, 1986).

15. Rosenfeld, *A Double Dying,* 27.

16. Andreas Huyssen, "Monument and Memory in a Post Modern Age," in James E. Young, ed., *The Art of Memory: Holocaust Memorials in History* (New York: The Jewish Museum, 1994), 16. For Nuchi, see *Natan Nuchi* (New York: Klarfield Perry Gallery, 1992).

17. These citations can be found in *Edith Altman: Photography/Text/Object* (Rockford: Rockford Art Museum, 1989); and *Kunst Arbeit* (Chicago: State of Illinois Art Gallery, 1992).

18. Ibid.

19. Lucy Dawidowicz, "Toward a History of the Holocaust," *Commentary,* 47 (April 1969): 56, cited in Alan L. Berger, *Crisis and Covenant,* 36.

20. Ann Poore, "'Jew' Exhibit Recalls Holocaust," *Salt Lake City Tribune,* 7 April 1991, sec. E, p. 1.

Maria Spitzer, b. 1904, Gyor,
Hungary, 1993
Photograph, toned gsp with
silver marker
16 x 20
Photo: Jeffrey Wolin and
Catherine Edelman Gallery,
Chicago

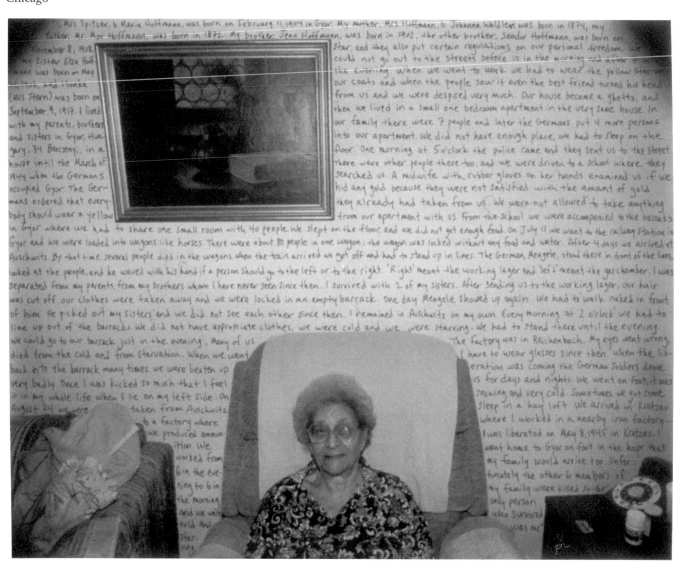

JEFFREY WOLIN

My interest in the Holocaust dates back to my childhood in the 1950s in a Jewish neighborhood in suburban New York. The war was still fresh in my parents' minds. My grandparents, immigrants from Eastern Europe, would go ballistic whenever talk would turn to Hitler and the Germans. My grandfather was unable to find out exactly what happened to his family, but they did not survive the war. I have spent the past two years engaged in my project with Holocaust survivors. Following an interview, I photograph them. I try to find elements in their stories that can be expressed visually in the portrait. I am fully aware that no one who did not directly experience the Holocaust can truly understand the depths of horror that Jews in Europe experienced at the hands of the Nazis. Nevertheless, it is my hope that by providing a face with an accompanying story of great power, an audience can empathize with the survivors.

LARRY RIVERS

"The greater part of the prisoners who did not understand German...died during the first ten to fifteen days after their arrival: at first glance, from hunger, cold, fatigue and disease; but after a more attentive examination, due to insufficient information. If they had been able to communicate with their more experienced companions, they would have been able to orient themselves better....Except for cases of pathological incapacity, one can and must communicate, and thereby contribute in a useful and easy way to the peace of others and oneself, because silence, the absence of signals, is itself a signal, but an ambiguous one, and ambiguity generates anxiety and suspicion. To say that it is impossible to communicate is false; one always can."

—Primo Levi, *The Drowned and the Saved*

Primo Levi: Witness Drawing, 1988
Pencil and color pencil on paper
26 ½ x 28 ½

The Last Journey, 1991
Collage
22 x 25

JUDITH GOLDSTEIN

I am a Holocaust survivor, born in Vilno (Vilna), Poland. In 1941, under the Nazi occupation, most Jews of Vilno were placed in the ghetto. About 50,000 Jews of the city were led to Ponar, a place in the forest outside Vilno, shot to death and thrown into pits. Most of my family are buried there. At the liquidation of the ghetto in 1943, I was shipped with my mother to concentration camps, Riga in Latvia, Stutthof and later Torun, Poland. There, I went through the tunnel of death, but survived by many miracles. My father never returned, my mother and brother survived. I am able to turn my experiences of horror and degradation into artworks. *The Last Journey* is from my memories of the Stutthof concentration camp. I saw these wagons with dead bodies taken to the crematorium.

Hidden Memories: Attic in Sastin,
1991
Acrylic on paper
60 x 120
Photo: Edward Owen

KITTY KLAIDMAN

Somehow, it seems to take about forty years for survivors to come to terms
with their personal Holocaust experiences. It took me just over forty years to
return to the places in western Slovakia where I was hidden as a child. Ever
since that trip, I have been working out my feelings about this part of my past
through images on canvas and paper.

   The paintings in this exhibition depict the dark hiding places in which I was
confined with my parents and brother. In each of these works, I introduced a
seemingly paradoxical infusion of light, which may represent the remarkable
fact that my immediate family survived intact. What it surely represents, however, is that the existence of people like Jan Velicky, the man most responsible
for saving us, serves as a beacon of hope in the most desperate times. For me,
being able to confront these spaces, as they are now and as I remember them,
made me realize the extent to which I have already made peace with my past.

NETTY VANDERPOL

I was thirteen when the Germans invaded Holland in 1940 and initiated the persecution and deportation of the Dutch Jews. I was forced to attend a school for Jewish children. One of my classmates was Anne Frank. In 1943 my father was imprisoned by the Nazis for having assisted Allied pilots who parachuted out of burning planes. He, my mother, my grandmother, my brother and I were sent to Westerbork, the last stop in Holland from which Jews were deported to various concentration camps. I spent over a year in Terezin in an increasingly desperate situation. When a rumor circulated that the Germans were looking for volunteers to be sent to Switzerland in an exchange for German POWs, we volunteered against the advice of most of the other inmates, who saw it as another trick. After a three-day train ride in February 1945, we crossed the border into Switzerland. This turned out to be the only exchange of Jews for German POWs. I have done needlepoint for many years. It was not until 1984 that I started my first piece that had the Holocaust as a focus. In this work, the number signifies the 257th person on the fifth transport from Holland; my number was my name.

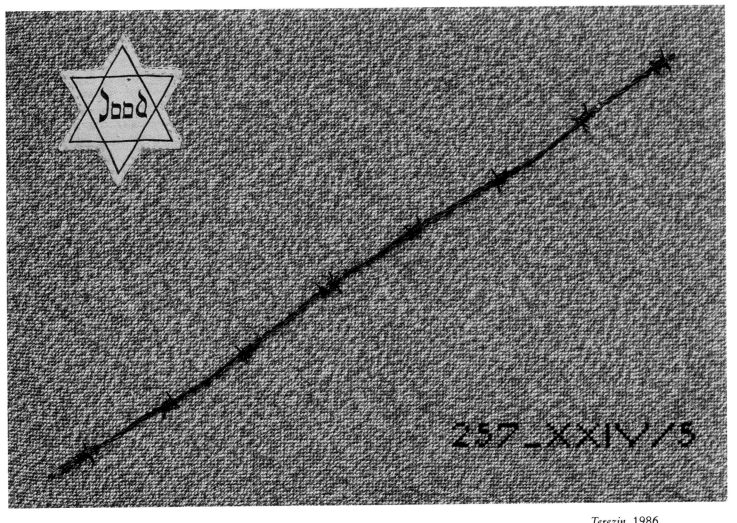

Terezin, 1986
Needlepoint
15 x 22
Photo: Clive Russ

ART SPIEGELMAN

Maus grew out of a comic strip I did in 1971 for an underground comic book: a three-page strip that was based on stories of my father's and mother's that I recalled being told in childhood....In 1977 I decided to do [a] longer work, [and] I set up an arrangement to see my father more often and talk to him about his experiences....Although I set about...to do a history of sorts, I'm all too aware that ultimately what I'm creating is a realistic fiction. The experiences my father actually went through [are not exactly the same as] what he's able to remember and what he's able to articulate of these experiences. Then there's what I'm able to understand of what he articulated, and what I'm able to put down on paper. And then of course there's what the reader can make of that....It's important to me that *Maus* is done in comic strip form, because it's what I'm most comfortable shaping and working with. *Maus* for me in part is a way of telling my parents' life and therefore coming to terms with it....It's not a matter of choice in the sense that I don't feel I could deal with this material as prose, or as a series of paintings, or as a film, or as poetry....In looking at other art and literature that's been shaped from the Holocaust—a historic term I find problematic—that material is often very high pitched....I feel a need for a more subdued approach, which would incorporate distancing devices like using these animal mask faces. Another aspect of the way I've chosen to use this material is that I've entered myself into the story. So the way the story got told and who the story was told to is as important [as] my father's narrative. To me that's at the heart of the work.

—From *Oral History Journal,* Spring 1987

Final Drawing for *Maus II*,
page 25, c. 1988–89
Ink on paper
9 ¼ x 6 ½
Copyright 1989 Art Spiegelman,
courtesy Galerie St. Etienne,
New York

GABRIELLE ROSSMER

Currently I am engaged in phase three of an installation work begun in January 1991. *In Search of the Lost Object* originally was shown at the Municipal Museum of Bamberg, Germany, a building that had been the *Judenhaus* where my grandparents were held until sent to their death in 1942 in Poland. Shown in Germany, the show was a memorial and an exploration of the layered nature of memory.

The initial challenge was the struggle to reconcile documentation with imagination. Specific references to members of my family in documents and images remain a central element in the pieces called *Document Wall* and *Family Portaits.* Images of my birthplace, Bamberg, appear like family members as well. Those pieces are shown in conjunction with cloth sculptures—*Les Revenants*—which are enigmatic shroudlike figures. The specific is the fuel that ignites the universal elements.

The recently completed *Garments,* hanging cloth sculptures that are twice life-size, are evocations of human form and style that are open to the interpretation of the viewer. An as-yet untitled piece consists of ninety-six plaster tablets with a variety of images connected by my life. Finally, there is a small autobiographical book that is the most "factual" element in the installation.

Reclaiming the Symbol/
The Art of Memory, 1988-1992
Installation
Dimensions vary

EDITH ALTMAN

When I was first born in Germany, I didn't speak the language; I saw only images. Then I came to America and, again, I didn't speak the language and saw only images. Images became symbols of experiences: the yellow star I wore, the swastika, the different languages, the different symbols in the Hebrew language that I studied as a child, the look of the German language and the biblical type that the Germans used in their propaganda art. *Reclaiming the Symbol* is the attempt to confront the symbols used by the Third Reich to empower and to terrorize. The work strives to reclaim the star, the cross and the swastika to their positive use. The swastika may well be the earliest known symbol, the solar wheel, the movement and power of the sun, the origin acting upon the universe, a positive symbol before the Nazis used it. By taking the swastika apart, by deconstructing its meanings and disempowering it, I hope to change its fearful energy. In a spiritual or mystical sense, I am exorcising the evil memory of the swastika, in hopes of healing our fear.

—From *Kunst Arbeit,* State of Illinois Art Gallery, 1992

JEROME WITKIN

The Nazis had so-called "brownhouses," and they would pull in Jews or Communists or people who were homosexuals and beat them to death. There was a whole litany of people being forced to watch somebody being killed or raped. Why these things happen and why people do these things, I don't know, but I think they tap into a kind of cultural madness. If this society continues to the next two thousand years, people will be looking at the twentieth century and saying, "What did artists do about the strange goings-on?"

—From gallery guide for Arnot Art Museum, 1992

The Beating Station, Berlin, 1933,
1989
Oil on canvas
36 x 132
Photo: Courtney Frisse

The Apotheosis of Krupp,
1988
Acrylic on canvas
72 x 64

ARNOLD TRACHTMAN

I was born in the United States, three years before the Nazis came to power in Germany. I was lucky. I grew up in the "Arsenal of Democracy." And yet it was not always safe. Anti-Semitism thrived here. At any time you could be attacked, verbally, physically or both, by kids your own age or older, and sometimes by adults. The end of the war came with newsreels of the camps and the infinite mounds of the dead being bulldozed into great pits. The survivors looked just barely alive. Their pain was palpable. When I found my direction as an artist, I made work about issues of the day. While pursuing these themes, I found my-self continuously drawn to the history of Nazism. Yet it did not appear in my work. I wasn't ready. In late 1985, I was. What I wished to do was demystify the demonology of Nazism. I wanted to show the men behind this great en-gine of genocide: the major industrialists and corporations of Germany, such as Thyssen, Krupp, Daimler, Benz, Siemens, to name a few. Ten years after the war, all of them were back in business. Understanding the epoch of Nazism, economically, politically and socially, is part of the unfinished business of our era. As this century draws to a close, aspects of Nazism are manifesting them-selves in various parts of the world. We must penetrate the darkness of our past in order to have a future.

DEBBIE TEICHOLZ

I was born to Eastern European Jewish survivors of the Holocaust. I grew up in the atmosphere of the Holocaust, living amid a plethora of personal accounts, Holocaust photographs and neurosis. I have chosen not to use archival images as symbols because I feel these images, which belong to our collective consciousness, often have a distancing effect on the viewer, because they are so recognizable and therefore emotionally dismissable. These images were photographed in Israel and Budapest in 1991 and 1992. They are intended to summon up associations of the Holocaust. As I smelled the freshly turned-over, rich, amber rows of Israeli earth, I thought about the rows of train tracks, and I still hear the silent screams. I walk through life with a displaced step, therefore I have chosen the triptych form to bear witness to the rhythm of the present-past-present time warp in which I travel daily.

Holocaust #15, 1991
Photos, acrylic,
lead on canvas
12 x 9
Photo: Todd Gieg

SUSAN ERONY

Although I grew up in a Jewish family, with a Russian father who lost four siblings in pogroms, was arrested twice and barely made it out of the country, the history of the Jews was not discussed in my home. I learned about the Holocaust while working in the civil rights movement. Almost thirty years later, I still wake up not knowing how I can be alive, comfortable and unafraid, when fifty years ago being Jewish was a death sentence for so many of my tribe. I spent three and a half years, from 1989 to 1993, focusing my artwork on the Holocaust and trying to answer my question: How can extreme discrepancies in the quality of existence be such a reality of the human condition? I went to Eastern Europe three times, photographing concentration camps, Jewish cemeteries and German steel plants. I collected remnants from Jewish synagogues in Poland. I talked to Jewish survivors, children of survivors, Polish Resistance fighters, Germans born after the war. The Holocaust is a touchstone in my life, a place to which I cannot avoid returning because there is no understanding it and I am not capable of abandoning the quest.

The Jews of Prague #13, 1992
Photos, acrylic, lead on canvas
10 x 8
Photo: Todd Gieg

Chimneys at Birkenau II from
Conversations with Rzeszow, 1991
Oil stick
43 x 60
Photo: Peter Lee

Mt. Oberg, Tofte, MN from
Conversations with Rzeszow, 1992
Oil stick
30 x 88
Photo: Peter Lee

JOYCE LYON

In *Conversations with Rzeszow,* I am engaged in a dialogue between the familiar and a place I knew initially only through fragmentary stories, silence and the efforts of my own imagination. Rzeszow is a small city in southeastern Poland, where my father grew up within an extensive Jewish community that was destroyed in World War II. As a child I was told little about the fate of my father's family; in recent years I have felt the need to know more. The dialogue in the work involves both images and text. There are several voices: my own, recounting and questioning my perceptions, and quotes from Primo Levi and Francine Prose, more knowledgeable sources, who recount and question theirs. Some of the drawings are about places in Poland: the endless fields of barrack chimneys I saw at Birkenau, a mass grave in the woods near Rzeszow. Others are places I know more intimately: a Minneapolis bird sanctuary, a summer home in upstate New York. The metaphor of place becomes a means to explore many kinds of knowing: one's own direct experience and its limitations, what can be intuited, what is possible to learn at a distance and what cannot, finally, be understood.

GERDA MEYER-BERNSTEIN

Shrine is an installation that honors the victims of the Holocaust by refusing to let their voices be silenced. In my native Germany, I lived through Kristallnacht and experienced severe violence and social upheaval. I left Germany in 1939 in one of the last children's transports to England; however, many of my family members perished.

Shrine evokes the claustrophobic environment of the cattle cars used by Nazis to transport their victims to the concentration camps. The claustrophobia is emphasized through repetition of photographs of the ovens on the left wall of the installation. On the right wall of the installation are photos of the infamous commander of the Auschwitz camp, Rudolph Höss. He was tried by the National Tribunal of Warsaw, found guilty and executed at Auschwitz on April 16, 1947.

I believe art has the power to change society. I want my work to provoke thought and debate in the viewer as well as an emotional response. No matter how painful the truth may be, it must be given a voice. Primo Levi's words still resonate today: "How much of the concentration camp world is dead and will not return? How much is back and coming back?"

In spite of the harsh reality of my work, it also addresses healing, hope and continuity. In a strange sense, the large photo of the Auschwitz oven on the back wall represents hope. People from all over the world travel to Auschwitz to pay tribute to the victims who died there. They place flowers in the ovens and light votive candles. These are the signs of life and hope for future generations.

Shrine, 1991
Installation
144 x 300

PEARL HIRSHFIELD

Billions of words have been published in books, periodicals and media since the end of World War II, including the widely circulated films and photos of the atrocities in the death camps and ghettos, but the enormity of all that happened during the Holocaust has yet to be explained. Each survivor's story, each victim's story, is different and I cannot get past the feeling, "It could have been me." In some way it was.

As a child, and as a first-generation American growing up in a vibrant Jewish community in Chicago, I felt protected and secure. With the early rumblings of Hitler, my world changed. I gradually became aware that anxiety and fear for loved ones left behind in Europe began to permeate my parents' lives and those of our immigrant neighbors. Letters from my father's parents and mother's relatives ceased abruptly at the beginning of the war. After my children were born, I continued the search for the missing pieces. It has become a quest for answers.

Shadows of Auschwitz is a walk-through installation constructed for viewers to enter, one person at a time. The numbers on the structure are tattoos sent to me by survivors who responded to the work-in-progress. Their names are inscribed on a separate scroll kept in a phylactery pouch. Other numbers are from the 1942–43 ledgers retrieved from Auschwitz.

As *Shadows of Auschwitz* is an ongoing work, numbers are continually added to the installation and names to the scroll as they are received. I continue to attempt to make sense out of this and other events through my work.

Shadows of Auschwitz, 1989
Installation
72 x 216

AFTER ALL (50 years later)

". . . only on the firm foundation of
unyielding despair, can the soul's
habitation be safely built."
Bertrand Russell, 1923

Me too,
        I would rather not look.

Too much familiarity,
my grandmother was
murdered.
In my body.

Zyklon gas was an improved
form of killing.
Do I,
like a drunk pleading to forget,
engage with the digital modernity?

TV brain lures
with stories and theories,
sensation when there is none.
The body is missing.

I work on TV, taming
it before it
lulls me. Each cut,
a wake to awake.

It takes repetition,
the killing was repeated.
Is repeated.
Over.

Pier Marton, 5754/1994

PIER MARTON

Jew, 1985
Installation with the
video *Say I'm a Jew*
Photos: Pier Marton
and Judah Magnes

*Schlafwagen: Who Will Say
Kaddish for Them?* 1994
Mixed media sculpture
60 x 24 x 24

MARLENE E. MILLER

I have chosen to make my sculptures from papier-mâché and put them in stage-like environments. In the past, I have worked with puppets in all facets of puppet theater. Supporting my intention to go this route was the ironic symbolism I found in the film *Shoah:* a survivor of Sobibor tells that under threat of death, the inmates were forbidden to refer to Jewish dead as "corpses" or "victims" or any term that suggested humanity. The Germans forced the inmates to call the bodies *figuren*—"puppets." This piece evolved after my extraordinary journey to Poland and Israel in 1992 with "March of the Living." Joining five thousand Jewish high school students, adults and survivors of the death camps, we paid tribute to the memory of six million European Jews who perished. Spiritual comfort is derived from saying the Kaddish, the Jewish prayer to cherish the memory of a deceased person. Entire families, however, were eradicated in the Holocaust. Who will say Kaddish for them?

#15 from *Wrappings,* 1984
Wood, burlap, paint and glue

SHIRLEY SAMBERG

When asked to write about my sculpture, it is always a dilemma. What to say?

With an artist it is always the material that speaks. When asked to create a stage set, I started gathering supplies. Burlap was one of the materials. It was very malleable and to me appealing. I had been welding at the time and needed a change. The challenge of using fabric with wood and earth elements appealed to me. The images seemed to spring from sources deep within me that I wasn't aware of. The dark and brooding sculptures took on a life of their own. I worked with a compulsion I didn't know I possessed. One figure emerged after another. Those who saw them were moved by the dark wellspring of grief. Grief for the loss of loved ones. Grief for the Holocaust. Grief for war, poverty and homelessness...and the list goes on....

Memorial, 1986
Oil on linen
39 ¼ x 31 ⅞
Photo: Shaun Provencher
Courtesy Pucker Gallery,
Boston

SAMUEL BAK

Shortly after the occupation of Vilna by the Wehrmacht, both of my grandfathers were taken to the Ponari forest and there they were shot, together with other Jews. On the following Yom Kippur holiday, both of my grandmothers were also taken to this forest. My father was shot by the Nazis a few days before the liberation of Vilna. I don't know how, of all people, my mother and I were selected by fate to survive the liquidation of the ghettos and the labor camps and the various hiding places in which we kept ourselves concealed during the German occupation. I feel the necessity to remember and take it upon myself to bear witness to the things that happened in those times, so that human beings today and those of tomorrow, if it were only possible, are spared a similar destiny on earth. So I have chosen the way of creating images of a seeming reality, imbuing them with a multitude of layers, from clear and unknown symbols to the most private and intimate feelings of a world that has its own apparent logic. I hope that the complexity of these paintings might go beyond my private story and beyond the vicissitudes that mark the Jewish people and their fate.

—From *The Past Continues,* Pucker Gallery, 1988

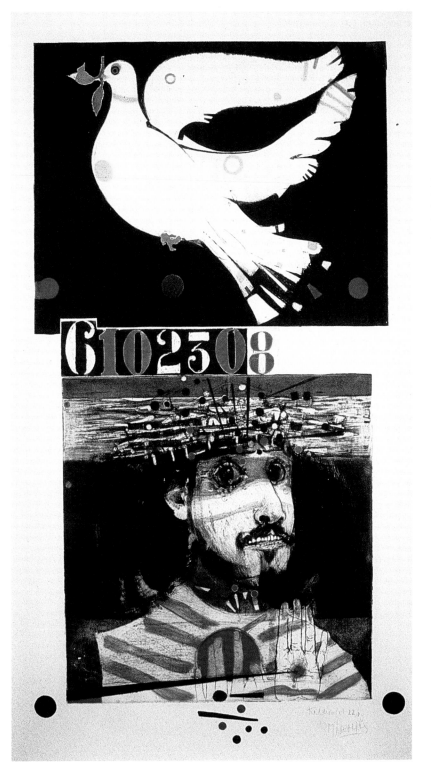

Kaddish #8, 1976
Intaglio print
45 ⅝ x 23 ⅝
Collection Minnesota
Museum of American Art

MAURICIO LASANSKY

Dignity is not a symbol bestowed on man, nor does the word itself possess force. Man's dignity is a force and the only modus vivendi by which man and his history survive. When mid-twentieth-century Germany did not let man live and die with this right, man became an animal. No matter how technologically advanced or sophisticated, when a man negates this divine right he not only becomes self-destructive, he castrates his history and poisons our future.

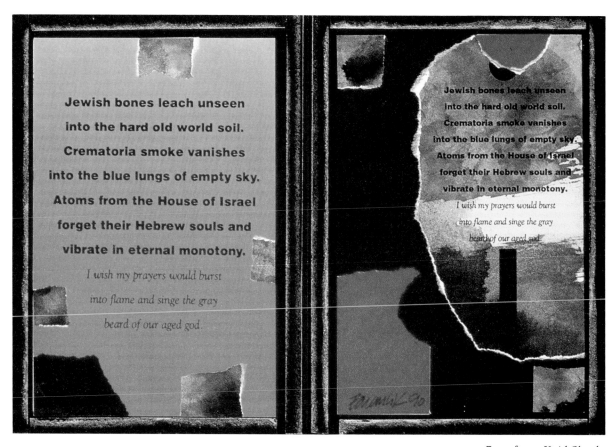

Page from *Kvitl Shoah:
Folded Messages,* 1990
Mixed media portfolio
7 x 9 ¾

ROBERT BARANCIK

The Shoah is past. What am I to make from my living Jewish flesh? Just before
my fortieth birthday, I was invited to the Vermont Studio Center as a visiting
artist and writer. It was the spring of 1990. The weather was bitter cold and
the snow dirty. The long Vermont mud season was beginning. I was given a
small, stark room with plenty of light and heat and the opportunity to work
without distractions for two weeks. What you see is the result of that intense
burst of study, prayer and artistic fury. These collages and *kvitls** were a cathar-
sis for the pain that I felt as a spiritual descendant of Jewish Holocaust victims.
The whole purpose of the "final solution" was to keep people like me from
being born. I have not done much "Holocaust Art" nor grieving since that fort-
night four years ago. Instead my wife and I have focused our energies on rais-
ing our only daughter as a religious American Jew and supporting the state of
Israel through the American Jewish Committee and Middle East Forum. Pres-
ently, I am working on a series of lyrical kvitls for a post-Holocaust Judaism and
new millennium.

*A kvitl is a small, folded message that highly religious Jews of Eastern Europe inserted
into the crevices of tombstones of great rabbis and sages. Kvitls often petitioned the
spirit of the departed or the Almighty to answer prayers or grant wishes.

MINDY WEISEL

My parents are survivors of the Auschwitz concentration camp. I was born in 1947 in Bergen-Belsen, Germany, in a displaced persons camp after the war. While growing up, I was told stories not only of the horrors of Nazi Germany and what my parents endured, but also of the beauty of their lives before the war. These paintings deal with the destruction of beauty as well as hope and survival. The numbers "A3146" are those on my father's arm from the camps; the color blue, my mother's favorite color, expresses the beauty and spirituality I was raised with.

CHECKLIST OF
THE EXHIBITION

All works "Collection of the Artist" unless otherwise noted.

Dimensions are in inches, height by width.

EDITH ALTMAN
*Reclaiming the Symbol/
The Art of Memory,* 1988-1992
Installation
Dimensions vary

SAMUEL BAK
Memorial, 1986
Oil on linen
39 ¼ x 31 ⅞
Collection of Pucker Gallery,
Boston

*Landscapes of Jewish History:
Ponar,* 1977
Charcoal on paper
33 ½ x 28 ½
Collection of Pucker Gallery,
Boston

Triptych, 1978
Oil on linen
63 x 144
Collection of Pucker Gallery,
Boston

Group With Blue Angel, 1973
Oil on linen
52 ½ x 39 ¼
Collection of Pucker Gallery,
Boston

ROBERT BARANCIK
Kvitl Shoah: Folded Messages,
1990
Mixed media
portfolio 8 x 5 ½

SUSAN ERONY
Holocaust #2, 1990
Photos, acrylic, lead on canvas
20 x 16

Holocaust #5, 1990
Photos, acrylic, lead on canvas
11 x 14

Holocaust #6, 1990
Photos, acrylic, lead on canvas
11 x 14

Holocaust #15, 1991
Photos, acrylic, lead on canvas
12 x 9

The Jews of Prague #13, 1992
Photos, acrylic, lead on canvas
10 x 8

The Jews of Lodz and Cracow #13,
1991
Photos, mixed media on canvas
10 x 8

Memorial to the Jews of Lodz #2,
1990
Found Hebrew text, acrylic, lead
on canvas
14 x 11

Memorial to the Jews of Lodz #3,
1992
Found Hebrew text, ashes,
acrylic, lead on canvas
14 x 11

The Building of the Temple, 1993
Photos, acrylic, xerox transfer on
canvas
44 x 44

JUDITH GOLDSTEIN
Vilno Ghetto, 1994
Collage
51 x 30

The Last Journey, 1991
Collage
22 x 25

The Crematory, 1994
Collage
33 x 12

PEARL HIRSHFIELD
Shadows of Auschwitz, 1989
Installation
72 x 216 floor space

KITTY KLAIDMAN
*Childhood Revisited:
The Journey II,* 1991
Mixed media on canvas
35 x 32

*Hidden Memories:
The Crawlspace,* 1991
Acrylic on paper
40 x 60

*Hidden Memories:
Attic in Sastin,* 1991
Acrylic on paper
60 x 120

MAURICIO LASANSKY
Kaddish #2, 1976
Intaglio print
44 ¹⁄₁₆ x 24 ⅞
Collection Minnesota Museum
of American Art

Kaddish #7, 1976
Intaglio print
44 ¾ x 24 ⅛
Collection Minnesota Museum
of American Art

Kaddish #8, 1976
Intaglio print
45 ⅝ x 23 ⅝
Collection Minnesota Museum
of American Art

JOYCE LYON
"Pliny" by Primo Levi from
Conversations with Rzeszow, 1991
Text panel
12 ½ x 10

*After I Saw "The Partisans of
Vilna"* from *Conversations with
Rzeszow,* 1991
Text panel
12 ½ x 10

*Later, in the New York Public
Library* from *Conversations
with Rzeszow,* 1991
Text panel
12 ½ x 10

Bird Sanctuary, Minneapolis I from
Conversations with Rzeszow, 1991
Oil stick
34 x 92

Chimneys at Birkenau II from
Conversations with Rzeszow, 1991
Oil stick
43 x 60

Mt. Oberg, Tofte, MN from
Conversations with Rzeszow, 1992
Oil stick
30 x 88

Mass Grave, Glogow, Poland I
from *Conversations with Rzeszow,*
1991
Oil stick
30 x 44

PIER MARTON
Jew, 1985
Installation with the video
Say I'm a Jew
Dimensions vary

**GERDA MEYER-
BERNSTEIN**
Shrine, 1991
Installation
144 x 300 floor space

MARLENE E. MILLER
*Schlafwagen: Who Will Say
Kaddish for Them?* 1994
Mixed media sculpture
60 x 24 x 24

LARRY RIVERS
Erasing the Past, 1986
Pencil and color pencil on paper
12 ½ x 10 ½

Erasing the Past II, 1986
Pencil and color pencil on paper
12 ½ x 10 ½

Primo Levi: Witness Drawing, 1988
Pencil and color pencil on paper
26 ½ x 28 ½

GABRIELLE ROSSMER
In Search of the Lost Object, 1991
Installation
Dimensions vary

SHIRLEY SAMBERG
#15 from *Wrappings,* 1984
Wood, burlap, paint and glue
Group of seven sculptures

ART SPIEGELMAN
Final drawings for *Maus II,*
Pages 23, 24, 25, 26, 27 and 28,
c. 1988-89
Ink on paper
24 x 30 (framed)

DEBBIE TEICHOLZ
Untitled from *Prayer by the Wall,*
1991
Photograph
35 x 64

Untitled from *Prayer by the Wall,*
1991
Photograph
35 x 64

Untitled from *Prayer by the Wall,*
1991
Photograph
35 x 94

Untitled from *Prayer by the Wall,*
1991
Photograph
35 x 94

ARNOLD TRACHTMAN
Peace in Our Time, 1991-92
Acrylic on canvas
98 x 60

Eastern Tours, 1989
Acrylic on canvas
84 x 60

The Apotheosis of Krupp, 1988
Acrylic on canvas
72 x 64

Our Most Important Product, 1987
Acrylic on canvas
71 x 50

NETTY VANDERPOL
Transports, 1985
Needlepoint
15 x 22

Terezin, 1986
Needlepoint
15 x 22

*Death is...Opa Mo, Oom Siegfried,
Jeannot...Three Out of
Millions,* 1986
Needlepoint
15 x 22

*"...And All the King's Horses and
All the King's Men..."* 1987
Needlepoint
15 x 22

MINDY WEISEL
Barbed Souls, 1980
Oil on paper
40 x 60
Private collection

The Drowned and the Saved, 1994
Oil on canvas with suitcase
66 x 78

Just, 1989
Oil on canvas
33 x 28

JEROME WITKIN
The Beating Station, Berlin, 1933,
1989
Oil on canvas
36 x 132

JEFFREY WOLIN
*Rena Grynbalt, b. 1926, Warsaw,
Poland,* 1993
Photograph, toned gsp with
silver marker
16 x 20

*Henryk Werdinger, b. 1923,
Boryslaw, Poland,* 1993
Photograph, toned gsp with
silver marker
16 x 20

*Jadzia Strykowska, b. 1924,
Tomaszow-Maz, Poland,* 1993
Photograph, toned gsp with
silver marker
16 x 20

*Josef Neumann, b. 1916, Snina,
Slovakia,* 1993
Photograph, toned gsp with
silver marker
16 x 20

*Heinz Katz, b. 1920, Homberg,
Germany,* 1993
Photograph, toned gsp with
silver marker
16 x 20

*Maria Spitzer, b.1904, Gyor,
Hungary,* 1993
Photograph, toned gsp with
silver marker
16 x 20

BIBLIOGRAPHY

Amishai-Maisels, Ziva. *Depiction and Interpretation.* London: Pergamon Press, 1993.

Art in a Concentration Camp: Drawings from Terezin. New York: New School Art Center, 1967.

Bak, Samuel. *Chess as a Metaphor in the Art of Samuel Bak.* Montreux, Switzerland: Olsommer, 1991.

___*The Past Continues.* Boston: David R. Godine, 1988.

Bernbaum, Israel. *My Brother's Keeper: The Holocaust Through the Eyes of an Artist.* New York: Putnam, 1985.

Blatter, Janet, and Sybil Milton. *Art of the Holocaust.* New York: The Rutledge Press, 1981.

Borowsky, Irvin J. *Confronting the Inconceivable.* Philadelphia: American Interfaith Institute, 1992.

Braham, Randolph L., ed. *Reflections on the Holocaust in Art and Literature.* New York: Columbia University Press, 1990.

Constanza, Mary. *The Living Witness—Art in the Concentration Camps and Ghettos.* New York: Macmillan, 1982.

Felstiner, Mary Lowenthal. *To Paint Her Life: Charlotte Salomon in the Nazi Era.* New York: HarperCollins, 1994.

Fluek, Toby Knobel. *Memories of My Life in a Polish Village, 1930-1949.* New York: Knopf, 1990.

Freudenheim, Tom L. "Viewing Holocaust Art as Art." *Shema: A Journal of Jewish Responsibility* 15/284 (December 28, 1984): 26.

Furth, Valerie Jakober. *Cabbages and Geraniums: Memories of the Holocaust.* Boulder: Social Science Monographs, distributed by Columbia University Press, 1989.

Gilbert, Barbara (curator). *From Ashes to the Rainbow: A Tribute to Raoul Wallenberg. Works by Alice Lok Cahana.* Los Angeles: Hebrew Union College Skirball Museum, 1986.

Goodman, Hannah Grad. "Survivors Reject Art History." *Shema: A Journal of Jewish Responsibility* 15/284 (December 28, 1984): 29.

Hilberg, Raul. "Conscience from Burlington." *Hadassah Magazine* (August/September 1991): 21-23.

The Holocaust in Contemporary Art. Exhibit at the Holman Hall Art Gallery, March 27-April 15, 1989. Trenton: Trenton State College, 1989.

Hunter, Sam. *Larry Rivers.* New York: Rizzoli, 1989.

Kampf, Avram. *Jewish Experience in the Art of the Twentieth Century.* South Hadley, Mass.: Bergin and Garvey, 1984.

Kitaj, R. B. *First Diaspora Manifesto by R. B. Kitaj.* London: Thames and Hudson, 1989.

Kushner, Marilyn. "Holocaust Art Is Testimony, Not Art." *Shema: A Journal of Jewish Responsibility* 15/284 (December 28, 1984): 27-28.

Lasansky, Mauricio. *The Nazi Drawings by Mauricio Lasansky.* Iowa City: University of Iowa Press, 1976.

Makarova, Elena. *From Bauhaus to Terezin: Freidl Dickler-Brandeis and Her Pupils.* Jerusalem: Yad VaShem, 1990.

Milton, Sybil. *In Fitting Memory: The Art and Politics of Holocaust Memorials.* Detroit: Wayne State University Press, 1992.

___*The Story of Karl Stojka: A Childhood in Birkenau.* Exhibition at the Embassy of Austria. Washington: U.S. Holocaust Commission, 1992.

Novitch, Miriam, and Lucy Dawidowicz. *Art from the Concentration Camps, 1940-1945.* Philadelphia: Jewish Publication Society, 1981.

Oppler, Ellen C. *Rico LeBrun: Transformations/Transfiguration.* Syracuse: Syracuse University School of Art, 1983.

Salmon-Livine, Irit. *Testimony Art of the Holocaust.* Jerusalem: Yad VaShem, 1986.

Saloman, Charlotte. *Charlotte: A Diary in Pictures.* New York: Harcourt, 1963.

Seeing Through Paradise: Artists in the Terezin Concentration Camp. Boston: Massachusetts College of Art, March 6-May 4, 1991.

Spiritual Resistance: Art from the Concentration Camps, 1940-1945. Philadelphia: Jewish Publication Society, 1981.

Terna, Fred. "Reflections of a Survivor/Artist." *Shema: A Journal of Jewish Responsibility* 15/284 (December 28, 1984): 28-29.

Thompson, Vivian Alpert. *A Mission in Art.* Macon: Mercer University Press, 1988.

Toll, Nellie S. *Behind the Secret Window: A Memoir of a Hidden Childhood during World War II.* New York: Dial, 1992.

Witkin, Jerome. *West '85: Art and the Law.* St. Paul: West Publishing Co., 1985.

Young, James T. *The Texture of Memory.* New Haven: Yale University Press, 1993.

Witness and Legacy was designed by Zachary Marell, composed by Interface Graphics, Inc. in Stempel Schneidler with display lines in Copperplate, printed by the John Roberts Company on Mountie Matte and bound by Muscle Bound Bindery, Inc. using the Otabind method.